What people are saying about …

I0798690

THE ARMORY OF LEADERSHIP

"I have led men for fifty-one years. I am continually amazed at how many men lack spiritual depth and find themselves living in the misty lowlands of mediocrity. All men long for a cause to die for, a challenge to embrace, and loved ones to protect. The problem is, few men know how to get there. Vince presents a compelling argument for living a godly life and how to cultivate a meaningful existence that honors the Lord. Unwrapping the Scripture with exceptional clarity, citing supporting examples, providing thought-provoking questions for reflection, and offering helpful suggestions leading to spiritual maturity will help you become a man after God's heart."

Greg Bourgond, DMin, EdD, adjunct professor at University of Northwestern and president and founder of Heart of a Warrior Ministries

"Vince Miller models his Resolute ministry to men with transparency, openness, honesty, and vulnerability. These are the keys to discipling and building godly men—and when we build godly men, everyone wins!"

Brian Doyle, president and founder of Iron Sharpens Iron

"Vince is living Hebrews 10:24 as he embodies what it means to spur one another on toward love and good deeds and to be ALL IN and bring God glory by living out our faith authentically and boldly! Vince's special sauce is his ability to hit right at the heart of challenges men face and drive our response as warriors in the fight as Christ followers and kingdom builders. I am a better man for knowing Vince and thank God for his genuine and Spirit-led focus on seeing men live to the fullest that God intended for us in this short time we have here on earth. Live All In!"

John Young, US Army veteran and leader of small groups in multiple churches across the US for over twenty years

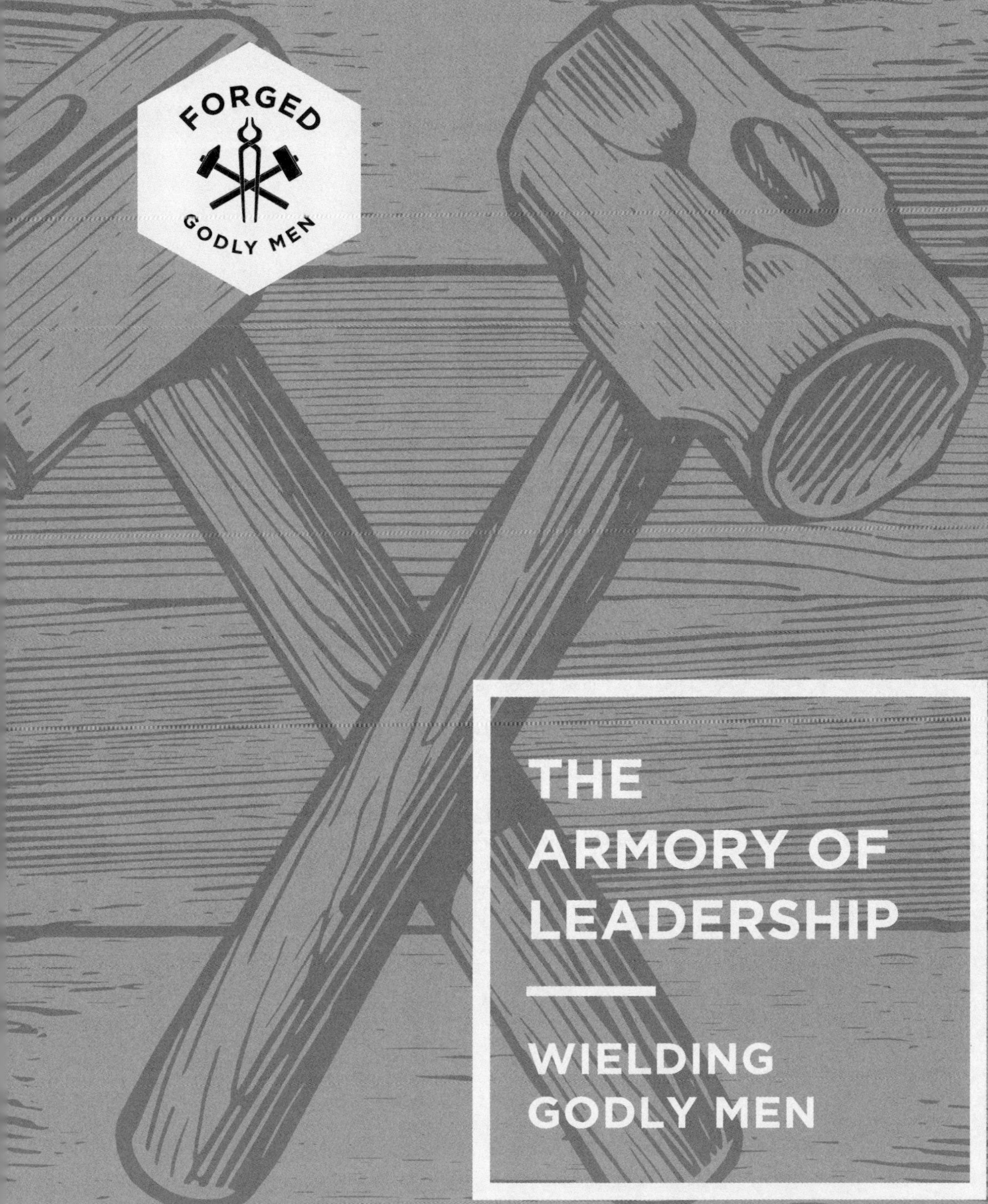

FORGED GODLY MEN

THE ARMORY OF LEADERSHIP

WIELDING GODLY MEN

150 YEARS STRONG
DAVID C COOK

THE ARMORY OF LEADERSHIP
Published by David C Cook
4050 Lee Vance Drive
Colorado Springs, CO 80918 U.S.A.

Integrity Music Limited, a Division of David C Cook
Brighton, East Sussex BN1 2RE, England

Library of Congress Control Number on file
ISBN 978-0-8307-8717-3
eISBN 978-0-8307-8718-0

The Team: Luke McKinnon, Jeff Gerke, James Hershberger, Jack Campbell, Karen Sherry
Cover Design: Micah Kandros

Printed in the United States of America
First Edition 2026

1 2 3 4 5 6 7 8 9 10

100625

I dedicate this book to the Christian man: the one who rises before dawn to face the day, knowing the battles ahead will be many. This is for the man who carries the weight of responsibility on his shoulders yet wonders if he's strong enough to bear it. It's for the man who feels the sting of failure but refuses to stay down, the man who prays in the quiet of the night when no one is watching, asking God for the strength to lead his family, his friends, his church, and his workplace.

You have been called to a noble task, and though the road is hard, know this: You are not alone. This journey you're on—the one where you question if you're enough, if you're capable, if you're worthy—it's the very road that will forge you into the leader God has called you to be.

This book is dedicated to you, the man who stays faithful even when the world pulls at him from every side. It's for the man who seeks to lead with courage, integrity, and a heart that beats for Christ, even when it costs him everything.

May this book be a tool in your hand, a source of strength when you feel weak, and a reminder that your leadership matters … more than you may ever know. Keep fighting, keep leading, and keep trusting that the One who called you is faithful. You are not just a man—you are God's man, forged in the fire for his glory.

CHAPTERS

To view an introductory video to this study, please visit https://beresolute.org/forged/.

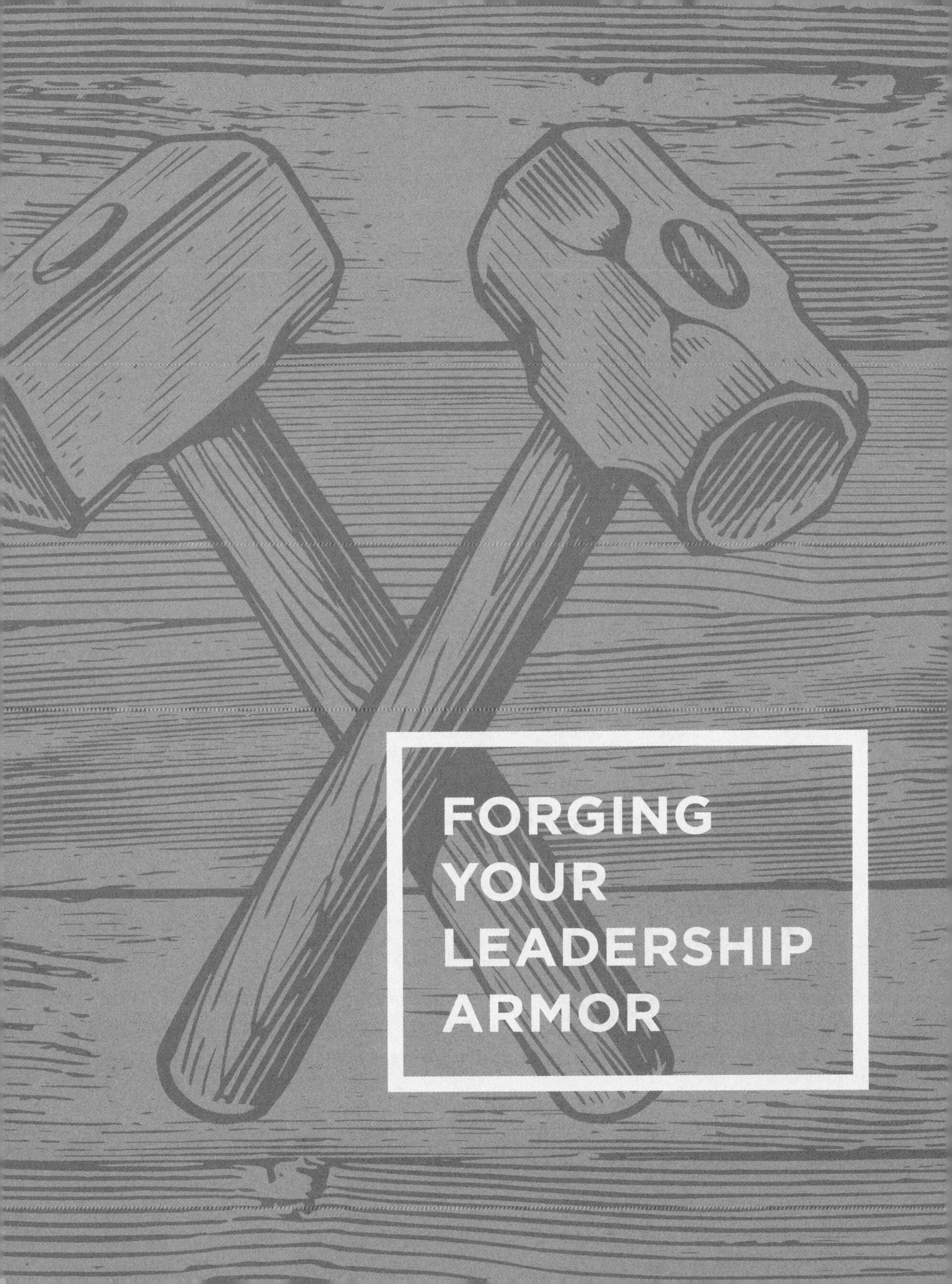

FORGING YOUR LEADERSHIP ARMOR

Equipping Yourself for the Battle Ahead

Leadership is not born in comfort; it is forged in the fires of life. Just as raw iron is shaped into a weapon of strength and precision, so too is the heart of a man refined and tempered for leadership. This process isn't passive—it requires the strike of the hammer, the fire of the forge, and the willingness to be shaped into something more substantial, sharper, and more useful for the kingdom of God.

In this book, *The Armory of Leadership*, you will embark on a journey to craft the tools you need to lead well in every sphere of your life. Each chapter will serve as an anvil upon which you will hammer out the principles of leadership, each forged from the truth of God's Word and refined through your daily experiences. As you work through these five chapters, you will be equipped with the spiritual weapons necessary to face the battles ahead.

Leadership is not born in comfort; it is forged in the fires of life.

We will begin by shaping the foundation of leadership: leading yourself. Like a sword being tempered in the fire, you must first surrender to the process of becoming stronger in your walk with Christ. Then, we'll move to the family, where the fire burns brightest and your leadership is tested daily. From there, we'll sharpen your leadership in the church and the workplace. Finally, we'll equip you to lead within your circle of influence, where your actions and presence matter most.

By the end of this journey, you will be a different man—one whose character has been refined, whose faith has been tempered, and whose leadership has been sharpened for the work of the Lord. You won't emerge from this armory as the same man who entered. You will be armed to lead with the confidence to wield the sword of faith and the tools to shape those around you for the kingdom of God.

This is not an easy path, but it is a noble one. The forge is hot and the work is demanding, but the result will be a man who is built for battle and prepared to stand firm and lead well in every area of life. So pick up your hammer, place the raw ore of your life on the anvil, and let's get to work. Together, we will build an armory that will not only shape your leadership but equip you to forge leaders for generations to come.

With that foundation in mind, let's begin by turning our attention inward. Leadership begins with the man himself. We'll start by exploring how to lead the most challenging person you'll ever face: yourself.

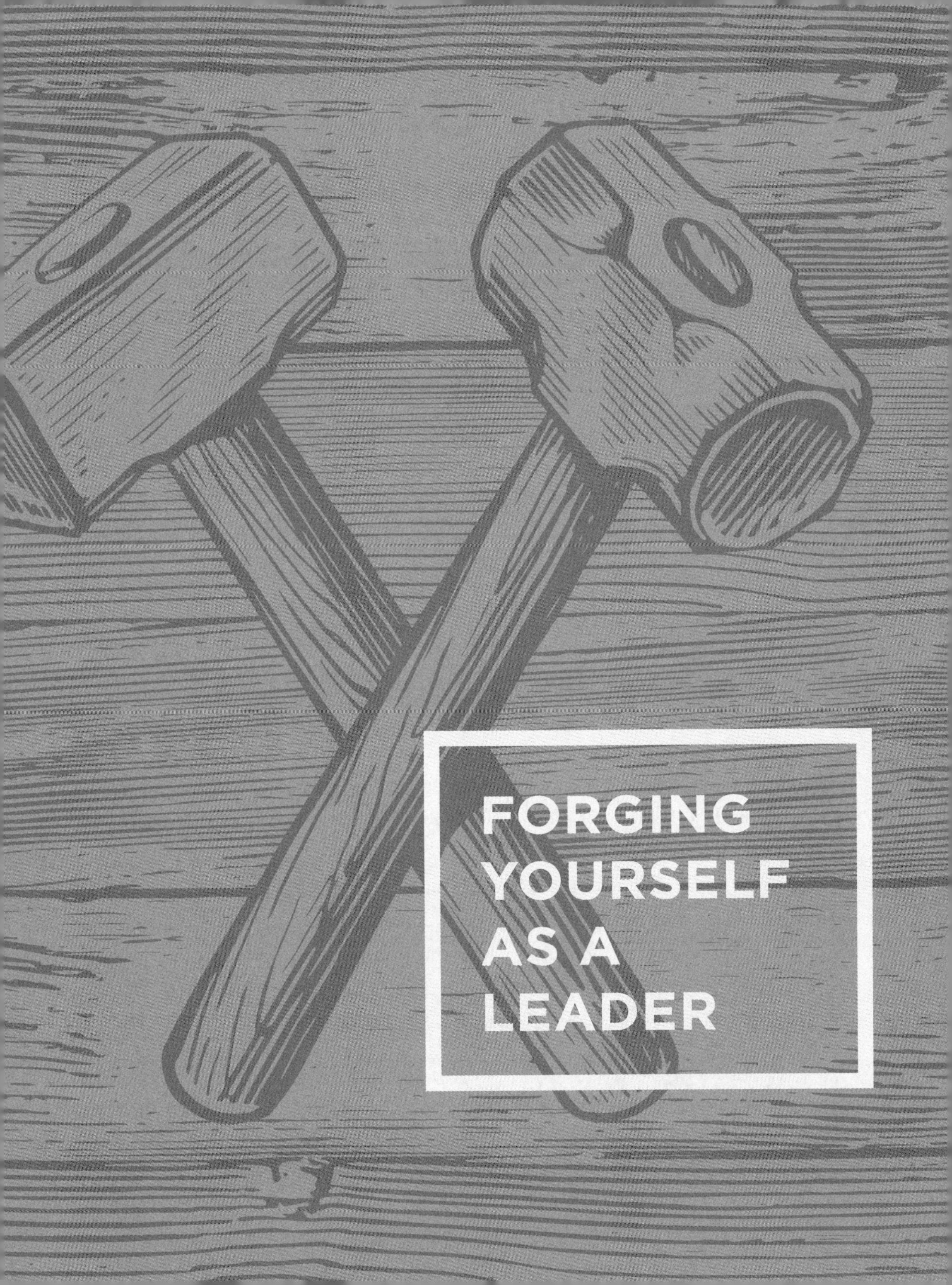

FORGING YOURSELF AS A LEADER

Leading Yourself

Leadership. It's a word tossed around in boardrooms, business books, and team meetings. Most people say it starts with self-awareness, skill development, and good training. And in a worldly sense, that's true—improve yourself well, and others may follow. But when it comes to spiritual leadership, that idea only scratches the surface.

Spiritual leadership (leading the way God intends) calls us to a different, more challenging road. The first person you will ever lead, and likely the hardest, is the one staring back at you in the mirror. This isn't a journey of self-discovery or self-promotion. It's not about becoming a better version of yourself. It starts with drawing a circle around your life and surrendering everything inside it. It's also not about *finding* yourself. It's about *dying* to yourself. You're not climbing a ladder. You're laying yourself down.

Here's the truth: If you can't lead yourself into complete submission to Christ, you can't lead anyone else—your family, your team, your church, or those in your circle of influence. True leadership in God's kingdom begins with a heart surrendered to the hands of the Creator. In this chapter, we will dig into what it means to lead yourself: how it looks, how it feels, and why it's essential to every other area of leadership in your life.

Brace yourself. This isn't leadership like the world defines it. It's deeper. It's harder. And it will change your life. If you're ready for this … really ready … it starts today, with you.

THE SINFUL INTENT OF MAN: WHY WE ARE HARD TO LEAD

When it comes to leadership, the biggest challenge isn't external, it's internal. The Bible bluntly reminds us of this truth in Genesis 6:5: "The LORD saw that the wickedness of man was great in the earth, and that every intention of the thoughts of his heart was only evil continually." This verse lays bare the nature of the human heart. While we may have ambitions to lead, even noble ones, God tells us plainly that our intentions are tainted by sin.

From the beginning, man's greatest struggle has been his own heart. We're prone to lead ourselves, and others, astray because the intent that drives us is corrupt. Our sinful nature affects every aspect of our leadership, making us difficult to lead, not only for others, but also for ourselves.

ONE | LEADING OURSELVES TOWARD SIN

But Genesis 6:5 doesn't stop at condemning the bad behavior. God also exposes the heart behind it. Every intention, every thought, was bent toward evil. Sin wasn't just something people stumbled into. They chose it. They led themselves there. This wasn't the occasional moral slip. It was a deeper issue—an inner bent pulling them away from God. A heart problem driving every decision.

It's also not about *finding* yourself. It's about *dying* to yourself. You're not climbing a ladder. You're laying yourself down.

As leaders in the home, the workplace, or the church, we carry our sinful inclinations into every sphere of influence. We may think we're pursuing noble goals, but if those aims are not fully surrendered to Christ, they remain self-directed. And direction apart from God is always self-directed and will drive us to drift toward sin.

This is why many men look successful on the outside yet feel hollow inside. Because leadership without submission to Christ isn't strength—it's rebellion dressed up as self-control.

TWO | LEADING WITH INTENT, THOUGHTS, AND HEARTS THAT ARE EVIL

Leadership is not an unbiased action. It flows from the heart. But this presents a serious problem: Our hearts are not always trustworthy. Scripture makes it clear that our hearts can easily mislead us. That's why godly leadership cannot depend solely on personal instincts or internal motivations. God's Word speaks directly to this issue:

> The word of God is living and active, sharper than any two-edged sword, piercing to the division of soul and of spirit, of joints and of marrow, and discerning the thoughts and intentions of the heart. (Heb. 4:12)

God sees beyond our words and actions. He examines our motives—those unseen intentions that drive our leadership. If our hearts are bent toward selfishness or sin, how can we possibly lead others, or even ourselves, toward what is right?

We can hide these intentions behind moral behavior or noble goals, but God knows our underlying motivation. Scripture reminds us that "the heart is deceitful above all things" (Jer. 17:9). This isn't about the occasional bad thought. It's about the condition of the heart apart from Christ—every thought, every desire, every motive, stained by sin. This is why spiritual leadership must begin with the surrender of the heart. Until God transforms the heart behind your leadership, you're just dressing up sinful ambition in spiritual clothes.

THREE | WE CANNOT LEAD OURSELVES OR OTHERS DOWN A RIGHTEOUS PATH

So, given the unrighteous impulse in our hearts, how can we possibly expect to lead others rightly? We can't even lead ourselves in the right direction! Thus, true leadership, in the biblical sense, isn't about control, influence, performance, skill, or behavior; it's about surrender. Our sinful nature disqualifies us from righteous leadership until we've submitted to God's authority.

True leadership, in the biblical sense, isn't about control, influence, performance, skill, or behavior; it's about surrender.

Paul echoed this truth when he said, "I know that nothing good dwells in me, that is, in my flesh. For I have the desire to do what is right, but not the ability to carry it out" (Rom. 7:18). This means that our leadership, when left to itself, will always be flawed. We can't lead others until we've been led by Christ. Only under his lordship can we guide others to him.

THE UNSEEN WOUNDS: FLAWS THAT WEAKEN THE BLADE

Let's look at five ways that sinful intent shows up in our leadership. Think of this like inspecting a blade before battle. These issues may vary in form, but each reveals a flaw—hidden weaknesses that resist God's refining fire.

Before leading others into spiritual battle, we must confront the sin that lies within our own hearts. Because no matter how sharp we look on the outside, if we are a weapon that is flawed on the inside, we will always fail under pressure.

ONE | SELF-RESISTANCE

The first common flaw in our leadership is self-resistance. It's that internal pushback we feel when we know what's right to do but don't do it. Our pride, fear, and stubbornness are the source of this resistance. That's why we bristle at being led by anyone, including God.

This is evident in how we neglect personal disciplines such as prayer, Scripture reading, and confession. We know we need these disciplines to stay sharp, but we resist the work they would do in us. Like a sword refusing the fire, we avoid the forge that could reshape us.

But this isn't just laziness. It's rebellion. We resist surrendering to anyone, including our God-given conscience and the Holy Spirit. That internal resistance is the first crack in the blade. And if we can't lead ourselves to overcome, how will we help others fight their own?

TWO | LOW SELF-AWARENESS

The second flaw is low self-awareness. We often miss the cracks forming in our own lives, even as we quickly notice the faults in others. Genesis 6:5

describes the depth of this issue: "Every intention of the thoughts of his heart was only evil continually."

That's a sobering statement. Yet how often do we pause to examine our intentions with that level of honesty?

Low self-awareness in leadership is dangerous. First, you can't repair what you won't admit is broken. Second, if you lead without addressing the cracks in your blade, you risk leading others into a losing battle. A leader who won't face his flaws is like a soldier charging into battle with a broken sword—bold but blind.

Godly leadership requires regular inspection. We must ask:

> *Are there cracks in my motives?*
> *Are there weaknesses that affect how I lead?*
> *Are there fires of refinement from God that I am resisting?*

THREE | EMOTIONAL BIAS

The third flaw is emotional bias. Our emotions, though real and often substantial, are unreliable guides. Left unchecked, they blur the line between God's will and our will. Thus, we may begin leading by *how we feel* instead of *what is true.*

When emotions lead, sin often follows. We become reactive, impulsive, or even manipulative, justifying our actions in the moment rather than anchoring them in the Word.

When emotions lead, sin often follows.

A blade driven by emotion will fail when put to the test. Leaders ruled by feelings are unstable, and instability in leaders injures those they lead. A man forged for God must be governed by truth.

FOUR | LACK OF SELF-DISCIPLINE

Lack of self-discipline is the fourth flaw because discipline is the edge of the blade. Without it, we're dull and unprepared for the spiritual demands of leadership. But here's the problem: Our sinful nature hates discipline, especially spiritual discipline. We prefer comfort over correction. We prefer ease over effort.

This flaw manifests in skipped prayers, half-hearted worship, or moral compromise. But leadership isn't built in the spotlight—it's forged in the daily, unseen grind. In the small choices that slowly shape a man.

Without discipline, men drift. And drifting men don't lead. They react, excuse, and rationalize. Discipline is what keeps us steady in the face of adversity. It proves that God, not our flesh, is leading us.

FIVE | INTERNAL CONFLICT

The final flaw is the war within. In Romans 7, Paul described the constant battle between what *we want to do* and what *we keep on doing*. Every man knows this battle. We desire to be righteous, but we keep falling short because we do something different.

This internal conflict is real and relentless. Pride wrestles with humility. Lust battles purity. Control fights against surrender. These aren't surface-level skirmishes. They're deep spiritual wars that reveal how much we still need God's refining grace.

We cannot lead ourselves out of this battle without God. Left alone, we'll swing wildly between guilt and pride, never walking in peace. But when we admit the conflict and bring it to God, he doesn't cast us out—he meets us at the forge and begins the work.

As we examine these flaws, one truth becomes undeniable: We are the most challenging people we will ever lead. Resistance, blindness, emotion, inconsistency, and inner war aren't just leadership challenges. They're heart issues. And unless we confront them with the fire of God's truth and grace, they will weaken everything we touch.

But here's the hope: The forge isn't a place of shame; it's where God reshapes us. And once he has forged us, we're ready to lead others into the fight.

REFLECTION AND DISCUSSION QUESTIONS

1. Which of the five flaws most affects your ability to lead? How might acknowledging these challenges foster growth in your spiritual leadership?

2. How can you surrender to Christ's authority? Is there something you need to confess and correct with God and others?

WHEN LEADERSHIP CRUSHED ME

I had some of my first leadership experiences in college. Like many young men, I was eager to prove myself, take charge, and make an impact in my fraternity, church, and campus organizations. Some of those experiences went well. I led a few projects that clicked, where everything came together, and I felt like I had nailed it. I thought, *This leadership thing isn't so hard!*

However, there were also other moments. Moments that crushed me. Situations where I felt out of control, where nothing I did seemed to work, and everything I tried made things worse. I walked away from those experiences thinking they were a failure of my skills. I wasn't prepared, didn't have the right strategy, and didn't know how to motivate people. At least, that's what I told myself at the time.

> **Spiritual leadership is far more about *mastering yourself* than *mastering skills.***

Looking back, I see now how blind I was. I thought I had a leadership problem. But it wasn't a skills issue—it was a soul issue. Those painful moments weren't the result of poor planning or a weak strategy. They exposed a deeper flaw: I didn't know how to lead myself. In college, I read the books, learned the frameworks, and mastered the techniques. I could rally people, inspire vision, and even manage outcomes. But no one ever told me that the hardest battle in leadership isn't on the outside; it's the one raging inside.

No amount of charisma could cover up the cracks in my character, and no clever tactic could compensate for a heart that hadn't been surrendered. I was trying to lead others while losing the war within.

And when the pressure came, I broke—not because I lacked skill, but because I had never been forged within as a leader.

You are the most difficult person to lead. Your sinful nature, pride, and desires trip you up far more than any external challenge. The Bible approaches leadership differently from what we often hear in the world. It starts with surrendering your heart, motives, and ambitions to God.

I wish someone had explained this to me back in college, which is why I'm telling you now. It probably would've saved me a lot of frustration. I thought leadership was all about mastering skills and influencing others, but spiritual leadership is far more about *mastering yourself* than *mastering skills*. And if you can't do that, you'll struggle to lead anyone else. I learned that the hard way, and maybe you have too. But here's the thing: The leadership lessons I was learning weren't just difficult; they were *counterintuitive*.

Most leadership books and conferences focus on skills—how to influence, motivate, and control. They feed into our natural desires for power, control, ambition, and self-sufficiency. It feels natural to pursue those things, and many leaders do. But as believers, we are called to a different kind of leadership. Spiritual leadership isn't built on *self-sufficiency*; it's built on *surrender*. It's not about control but submission to God's authority.

Everything I thought I knew about leadership collapsed in that season. I had built my confidence on plans, performance, and personal drive. But God wasn't calling me to become more effective. He was calling me to become more surrendered.

Spiritual leadership turned everything upside down. It wasn't about pushing harder. It was about letting go. Not rising to the top, but laying myself down. Not creating something for myself, but allowing God to make something in me.

He wanted self-denial instead of self-promotion. He wanted servanthood instead of ambition. He wanted dependence instead of control. These are not the lessons the world teaches leaders, but they are the truths God uses to forge them. As I said, they are *counterintuitive*.

That's when I began to understand that leadership doesn't start with external action; it starts with internal work done in the forge with God. God had to take the raw, unrefined parts of me and put them to the fire. He wasn't sharpening a sword. I was the sword. And I wasn't ready to be wielded until I surrendered to the heat.

Spiritual leadership is not about taking control; it's about surrendering it.

If you want to lead spiritually, you must think differently. You must be willing to be melted in the fire and molded by the anvil with the hammer of God. Spiritual leadership is not about taking control; it's about surrendering it.

I wish someone had told me this thirty years ago.

However, the four truths that follow are even more compelling. These four forge points can reshape your understanding of leadership. They are the lessons I learned on the anvil of God, and I believe they'll challenge everything you've ever been told about leadership.

REFLECTION AND DISCUSSION QUESTIONS

1. Can you recall times when your leadership felt more like a struggle? How do these moments highlight the need to lead yourself before leading others?

2. In what areas are you resisting God's authority? How can adopting a mindset of servanthood and self-denial transform your leadership approach, both personally and in interactions with others?

FORGED FOR LEADERSHIP: FOUR TRUTHS THAT SHAPE YOUR LEADERSHIP

ONE | SURRENDER

Spiritual leadership doesn't start with greatness. It starts with a grave. Before God builds a man, he breaks him. And the first blow to the old self is surrender.

The Crucified Leader

Surrender always sounds like weakness. Like giving up. Like losing control. And that's exactly why it makes us uncomfortable. But in God's kingdom, that's where authentic leadership starts—not in asserting authority, but in relinquishing it.

Paul captured this eloquently when he said, "I have been crucified with Christ. It is no longer I who live, but Christ who lives in me" (Gal. 2:20). Crucifixion isn't symbolic—it's real and complete. It's not a tweak to behavior or a subtle motivational shift. It's death to the man and leader you used to be.

In the same way that Christ physically died for our sins, we are called to spiritually die to our sinful desires, selfish ambitions, and pride. That's not easy, but it's essential. Because until the old man dies, the new man can't live. Until the weapon is melted, it can't be reforged.

The Furnace of the Forge

Just consider the forge. You don't forge a sword by polishing rusted steel—you melt it down. You expose it to the heat, burn away what's impure, and shape it into something new. That's what surrender is: the heat that softens pride, breaks self-will, and removes self-dependence.

God doesn't want to improve the old version of you. He wants to crucify it. He's not forging leaders who are impressive on the outside but hollow on the inside. That would be pharisaical and inconsistent. He's building men who are refined in fire. Men who are useful in his hands. And it starts by handing him everything.

This is the paradox of spiritual leadership. We gain power not by asserting ourselves but by surrendering. We lead by dying. By laying down our desires so that Christ's desires can reign in us. This is counterintuitive to everything we've ever learned about leadership.

The Cross Isn't for Wearing but for Dying

When Paul used the word "crucified," he wasn't speaking poetically. He was addressing the daily death of ego, entitlement, and control. Crucifying the old self isn't a onetime moment—it's a continual act of surrender.

There's a reason Jesus said, "Whoever does not take his cross and follow me is not worthy of me" (Matt. 10:38). You can't carry the cross and your ego at the same time. One has to go.

You can't carry the cross and your ego at the same time. One has to go.

This is why Paul emphasized the need for crucifixion. There is no resurrection without death. There is no new life in Christ without first laying down the old one. The same principle is true for leadership. You can't lead in God's way if you're still living your way. The two ways are incompatible.

Power in Powerlessness

Here's the strange truth that most leaders fail to learn: The more you surrender, the stronger you become. The more you let go of your plans, the more God's plan is revealed. As you die to yourself, Christ comes alive in you.

Surrender is not a passive activity either. It's internal warfare. It's not a loss of identity. It's the death of an identity that rebels against God. And in that surrender, Christ doesn't just lead you—he leads through you.

Until Christ is the one living in you and leading through you, you're just secretly managing your private rebellion. Authentic leadership flows from the life of Christ, not from human effort.

Death to the Old Man

When it comes to leadership, you don't need a better leadership model—you need to become a different man. That begins with death, not to your passion for leading, but to the patterns, pride, and hidden motivations that lead you away from God.

Spiritual leadership isn't about finding a better method; it's about dying to yours so God's way can take over. He doesn't anoint plans. He anoints surrendered men.

Before God anoints you with authority, he requires your allegiance. Before he puts a sword in your hand, he puts you in the fire.

Lay it down. Let him melt you. Only then can he mold you into a man worthy of his mission.

REFLECTION AND DISCUSSION QUESTIONS

1. What part of your old self are you still trying to manage instead of crucifying? How is that affecting your leadership?

2. If God uses only surrendered men, what's one area of your life you need to lay down today so he can lead through you?

TWO | SELF-DENIAL

If surrender is the death of the old man, then self-denial is the discipline that keeps him buried.

The flesh doesn't stay down without a fight. Even after we surrender, our self-centered desires rise up day after day to reclaim control. They whisper in moments of stress, temptation, or comfort:

> *You've earned this.*
> *You deserve that.*
> *Don't deny yourself now.*

Jesus gives us no room for compromise on this matter. "If anyone would come after me, let him deny himself and take up his cross daily and follow me" (Luke 9:23). This isn't a motivational adage; it's our marching orders. And if we're going to lead others spiritually, we must first learn to lead ourselves in the art and practice of consistent self-denial, because leadership without self-denial always becomes self-serving.

If surrender is the death of the old man, then self-denial is the discipline that keeps him buried.

The Inner Revolt

The self never wants to be denied. It wants to be indulged, praised, respected, and obeyed. That's why leadership is dangerous ground. If we don't crucify our craving for admiration or influence, it will quietly twist our leadership into something self-serving.

We can spiritualize it. Mask it. Justify it. But no matter how noble we make it sound, if our motive is to serve ourselves, we're not leading for God. We're leading for the glory of our name, not his (John 7:18).

Self-denial is the spiritual discipline that checks the inner revolt. It's the act of telling yourself no when your flesh screams yes. It's choosing the narrow road, the quiet place, the harder way—not because you must prove anything, but because that's the path Christ walked.

The Fight for First Place

At its core, self-denial is about who's first. It's not about saying no to chocolate cravings during Lent or skipping a Netflix binge for personal benefit. It's about choosing Christ when your comfort, your calendar, and your cravings all want to be king.

Every day, there's a tug-of-war for the throne of your heart. The self wants one thing, but Jesus demands another. Spiritual leaders understand this tug-of-war and make the hard call, not the easy one, every day. When we deny ourselves, we're not just exercising discipline. We're declaring that Jesus is better than whatever else we want at that moment.

And here's the danger: If we don't practice daily self-denial in private, we'll make selfish decisions in public leadership. Men who can't say no to themselves won't be able to say yes to God's call when it costs them something.

The Long Obedience in the Same Direction

Self-denial isn't flashy. It's not inspirational Instagram content. It's not often rewarded or recognized. It's quiet. Unseen. Repetitive.

But that's what makes it so powerful.

The world celebrates ambition and self-fulfillment. But Jesus calls us to die again and again. Spiritual leadership is forged in the slow, silent, steady grind of obedience. It's forged when you get up early to pray instead of sleeping in or scrolling on your phone. When you serve without thanks. When you choose integrity over opportunity. When you do the right thing and no one applauds.

This is how leaders are made—through long obedience in the same direction. Not big, dramatic moments, but the thousands of daily deaths to self that no one else sees.

Feeding What Matters Most

You can't kill the self by accident. It has to be starved.

You starve your flesh by feeding your spirit. You deny your flesh by indulging in God's Word, in prayer, in worship, in service. The man who walks in the Spirit "will not gratify the desires of the flesh" (Gal. 5:16). But you can't walk in the Spirit if you're still feeding and fueling the flesh.

Self-denial is not exclusively about deprivation. It's also about direction. You're not just turning away from something; you're turning toward Someone. The goal isn't willpower—it's worship. It won't win you praise, and it definitely won't go viral, but it will make you holy. It will make you the kind of man God can trust with influence.

Self-denial is not just turning away from something; you're turning toward Someone.

Your flesh will never stop seeking attention. But you can stop giving it power. Every day you deny yourself, you are saying with your life, "Jesus is worth more than what I want right now." That's not weakness. That's leadership.

REFLECTION AND DISCUSSION QUESTIONS

1. In which areas of your daily life are you most tempted to prioritize your comfort or desires over God's call?

2. What one habit could you change this week to feed your spirit and starve the self that still wants control?

THREE | SUBMISSION

Every man wants to lead with confidence. To speak with clarity. To make decisions and move forward with purpose. But in spiritual leadership, authority doesn't come from force. It comes from alignment.

That's what submission is—it's not passivity. It's not losing power. It's placing yourself under God's power. And that's where real leadership begins.

Jesus said, "Whoever does not take his cross and follow me is not worthy of me" (Matt. 10:38). This isn't just a statement about sacrifice. It's a call to alignment with his will. He didn't say, "Chart your own path" or "Lead in your own name." He said, "Follow me." That means he leads and we follow. We get in line.

If you're not aligned with Christ, you're not leading; you're drifting. You might even be leading people astray.

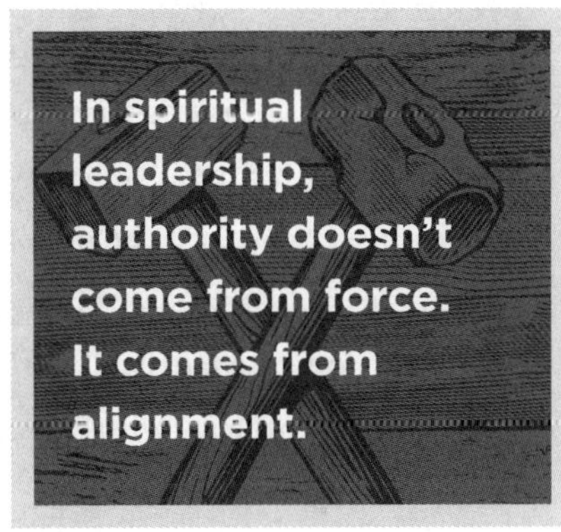

Authority from Alignment

In the kingdom of God, submission is not weakness—it's where strength is transferred. You don't carry weight just because you have a position. You carry weight because you're walking under permission.

That's the way Jesus lived. Though equal with the Father, he submitted fully to the Father's will (John 6:38). His words, his miracles, his authority … it all flowed from alignment.

The same is true for us: You can't lead in God's power if you ignore God's voice. You can't represent his name if you're still promoting yours.

Submission is not stepping down from leadership. It's stepping into leadership knowing the right order.

Stewards, Not Sovereigns

The parable of the talents (Matt. 25:14–30) makes it clear that the things God has given us to lead, we don't even own. The servants in that story weren't given authority to do whatever they pleased. They were entrusted with their master's resources to manage and multiply what didn't belong to them.

That's what submission looks like. Everything we have, our gifts, influence, opportunities, belongs to God. We are not sovereign rulers; we are stewards under orders. And our job is not to innovate our own mission but to be faithful to his.

> **Our job is not to innovate our own mission but to be faithful to his.**

When you embrace submission, you lead with humility. You stop trying to prove something and start trying to be faithful. And that's the kind of leadership God honors.

Misalignment Always Costs

A man out of alignment with God will always lead others into confusion. When we ignore God's Word or resist his Spirit, we lose clarity. We start making decisions based on pressure, pride, or insecurity, and the people we lead pay the price.

Just like a car that's out of alignment pulls to one side, a leader out of alignment veers off course. The longer we drive like that, the more damage we do to ourselves and others.

If you want to lead with integrity, you must check your alignment.

> *Are your plans submitted to prayer?*
> *Are your goals surrendered to Scripture?*
> *Are your decisions rooted in obedience?*
> *Or are you only aligned with the needs of your ego?*

The Freedom of Following

There's a strange freedom that comes when you finally let go of the illusion of control. When you stop trying to be the hero. When you stop carrying the pressure to figure it all out. When you stop pretending that success depends on your brilliance.

That's what submission does: It lifts the burden of leadership off your shoulders and places it where it belongs—on God. He never asked you to lead alone. He asked you to follow faithfully.

Submission isn't losing freedom. It's gaining direction. And when you're under God's authority, you start leading others with the confidence of someone who knows who's really in charge.

You don't have to build your own kingdom. You don't need to carry the pressure of getting it all right. You're not the point—Jesus is.

True spiritual leadership isn't about climbing the ladder of power. It's about kneeling in obedience. When you align yourself under Christ's authority, his power flows through you, and that's leadership worth following.

REFLECTION AND DISCUSSION QUESTIONS

1. Where in your leadership are you most tempted to rely on your own control instead of God's authority?

2. What's one decision you need to surrender right now to get back in alignment with Christ?

FOUR | SERVANTHOOD

In our world, leaders chase visibility. They want the spotlight, the platform, the title. But in God's kingdom, greatness doesn't come from standing above others—it comes from kneeling to serve them.

That's what set Jesus apart. Though he had every right to demand worship, he wrapped a towel around his waist, knelt down, and washed dirty feet. Then he said to his disciples, "I have given you an example, that you also should do just as I have done to you" (John 13:15).

That wasn't just an act of humility. It was a declaration of identity. Jesus, the King of Kings, chose the position of a servant and said, "This is what leadership looks like." If servanthood was enough for the Son of God, it must be more than enough for us.

The Identity Beneath the Title

In Romans 1:1, Paul opened his letter with a striking introduction: "Paul, a servant of Christ Jesus, called to be an apostle." He led with his true identity, not with the title of apostle, not church planter, not leader. But servant.

That order matters. Before Paul had a role, he had a posture. Before he had influence, he had surrendered. "Servant" wasn't just a title for Paul—it was his identity. He didn't serve because he had to. He served because he belonged to Christ.

Before Paul had a role, he had a posture.

That's the call for every man who wants to lead spiritually. Before you try to lead others, before you carry the weight of influence, you must settle this: Do I see myself as a servant first? If the answer is no, your leadership is already off course.

The Security of a Servant

Many men avoid servanthood because they think it makes them look small. But the truth is, it makes you secure. When your identity is rooted in Christ—not in your title, success, or image—you stop needing applause to feel validated.

The world says you're only as good as your latest win. But God says you're his even when you fail. Servants don't strive to impress; they aim to be faithful. And this changes how we lead. We no longer lead from insecurity or ego. We lead from a settled strength—because we know who we belong to and what he's called us to do.

Towel Before Titles

John 13 gives us the most vivid picture of leadership in all of Scripture. Jesus, fully aware that the Father had given him all authority, took off his robe, picked up a towel, and began washing his disciples' feet.

Let that sink in: Jesus had all authority, and he chose to serve. That wasn't symbolic. It was strategic. He redefined leadership. For him, leadership was not a position to wield but a towel to carry.

And this is where true leadership begins. You don't earn influence by demanding respect. You earn it by serving when no one's watching. By doing the unnoticed, uncelebrated work.

The Unshakable Foundation

Here's why servanthood is so important: It's the only leadership identity that cannot be taken from you.

Positions change. Titles are lost. Roles come and go. But if your identity is rooted in being a servant of Christ, you're grounded in an eternal identity. I believe this is why Paul could endure beatings, rejection, and prison and still write with boldness. His role didn't define him. His relationship with Christ did.

Leadership built on status will collapse under pressure. But leadership built on spiritual servanthood under the authority of Christ is unshakable. Because it's not about you. It's about him.

Leadership is not about climbing higher—it's about bending lower. Jesus didn't lead from a throne. He led from a basin. And when we take up the towel, we follow in his steps. So let the world chase influence. But you chase faithfulness. Serve when it's unseen. Sacrifice when it's inconvenient. Lead from your knees.

Because the lowest place is often where the highest impact begins.

THE ARMORY OF LEADING YOURSELF

So here is what we have learned in this chapter.

Spiritual leadership doesn't start with leading others. It starts with being led by Christ. And that kind of leadership isn't built on charisma, gifting, or titles. It's forged in fire. God uses the flames of formation to shape men into weapons for his purposes. Not through worldly tactics—but through four foundational truths: Surrender, Self-denial, Submission, and Servanthood. Remember:

> **Surrender** melts the mold.
> **Self-denial** refines the iron.
> **Submission** shapes the metal.
> **Servanthood** sharpens the blade.

These four truths don't compete; they work together. They strip away pride, shape our purpose, and prepare us for battle. In a world chasing status, God is still forging faithful, surrendered men—men ready for his mission.

Here's the charge to go with these four truths:

> *Go low.*
> *Die daily.*
> *Follow closely.*
> *Serve boldly.*

Let God forge you into a man who doesn't just lead but leads like Jesus: refined by fire, shaped by surrender, and ready for battle.

Now that we've forged the foundation of personal leadership, it's time to bring that fire home. Because the home isn't just where we live—it's where our leadership is most visible, most tested, and most impactful. That's where the next battle begins.

REFLECTION AND DISCUSSION QUESTIONS

1. Where are you tempted most when it comes to these four truths?

2. What action do you most need to address immediately: go low, die daily, follow closely, or serve boldly?

FORGE YOUR CONDUCT: A DAILY REFLECTION

Exercise: For a week, take five minutes each morning to reflect on your conduct. Consider the upcoming interactions you'll have (work, family, social settings) and set a goal to respond with integrity and godliness in those situations. At the end of the day, review how you did. Did your actions align with Christ's example? What can you improve tomorrow? Do you need to go ask for forgiveness today?

Only let your manner of life be worthy of the gospel of Christ. (Phil. 1:27)

FORGING THE FAMILY LEGACY

Leading Your Family

BUILDING THE HOMEFRONT

Family leadership is one of the greatest tests of a man's strength and one of his greatest callings.

If you're not married or don't have kids yet, don't check out. This chapter isn't just for husbands and fathers. It's preparation for the man you're becoming. Spiritual leadership in the home doesn't begin with a wedding or a birth certificate. It begins in private, when no one's watching. In the quiet choices. The daily disciplines. The pursuit of God long before anyone follows your lead.

And make no mistake, leading at home is more complex than leading anywhere else.

Why? Because there's no hiding.

Your family sees you unfiltered.

They've watched you lose your cool, forget promises, and wrestle with doubt. They've seen the best and the worst of you. There's no pedestal at home ... just people who know you deeply. That familiarity makes leadership more vulnerable, more humbling, and far more important.

It's easy to lead where you wear armor—things like titles, status, and outward success. But at home, the armor comes off. Titles mean little. What matters is character, consistency, and spiritual courage.

In that crucible, real leadership is forged.

And here's the truth: Of all the titles you'll wear in life—boss, coach, mentor, friend—three will echo into eternity.

Disciple. Husband. Father.

Each one is shaped in the furnace of the home. That's where your legacy is forged. That's where leadership becomes real.

No man comes into this world knowing how to lead a family. But every man of God is called to learn. And it's not only possible, it's necessary. Leading your home God's way leads to joy, purpose, and a legacy that ripples through generations.

In the pages that follow, we'll explore why so many men feel unprepared to lead spiritually at home, and we'll see how you can rise above passivity, pick up your tools, and build what matters most.

FOUR REASONS MEN DON'T LEAD AT HOME

WHY YOU CAN'T AFFORD TO STAY ON THE SIDELINES

Let's be honest: Spiritual leadership at home can feel overwhelming. Your schedule is packed. Work drains your energy. Family dynamics get messy. And when you finally get a quiet moment, leading spiritually might feel more like a burden than a calling.

But here's the truth: This isn't optional.

God has called you to lead your home. Not perfectly, but intentionally. Not with every answer, but with growing faith.

Many men hesitate because they feel unqualified, unprepared, or unsupported. However, the absence of leadership leaves a gap, and gaps always get filled. Sometimes by silence. Sometimes by stress. Sometimes by someone who was never meant to carry that weight alone.

In the next few pages, we'll confront the four most common reasons men hold back. And we'll expose them for what they really are: not obstacles, but opportunities for growth.

If you've been sitting on the sidelines, this is your moment to step onto the field.

ONE | HABITUAL SIN

"I'm too sinful to lead my family spiritually."

This may be the most common excuse men give for avoiding spiritual leadership. And on the surface, it almost sounds noble. You don't want to be a hypocrite. There's a sin you haven't conquered yet, and shame tells you to stay silent. You think, *If I still struggle, how can I possibly lead?*

But let's be clear. Struggle doesn't disqualify you. Silence does.

The presence of sin in your life doesn't mean you can't lead. Only Jesus was sinless! No, sin in your life means you must lead with dependence. Sin is not the reason to step back—it's the reason to step forward with humility.

Yes, ongoing, unrepentant sin will sabotage your influence. Your family sees it. Even if they can't name it, they feel it. But the answer isn't pretending or disappearing. It's confession and change. It's choosing to fight instead of freeze.

Spiritual leadership isn't about sinlessness. It's about surrender. It's not about pretending to be perfect. It's about showing your family how to pursue grace in real time.

Your wife and kids don't need to see a flawless man. They need to see a man who is honest about his battles, who owns his failures and keeps getting up again.

The difference between a man who leads well and one who doesn't is not perfection but *repentance.*

It's the willingness to go to war with your sin for the sake of those you love.

Your family can follow that kind of man.

TWO | NO ROLE MODEL

"I never saw spiritual leadership modeled for me."

For many men, this is a deep wound. You didn't have a father who showed you how to pray, lead with faith, or walk humbly with God. Maybe your dad was physically present but spiritually absent. Or maybe he caused pain instead of pointing the way.

So, now as a husband or father, you feel unprepared. Like a man given a sword but never trained to use it. Leadership feels awkward. Unnatural. Heavy.

But a missing role model is not an excuse to stay passive. It's a call to start something new.

David didn't inherit a godly legacy from King Saul. And Timothy's father offered little spiritual guidance. Yet both rose to leadership, not because of their upbringing, but because God called them, and he provided faithful mentors along the way.

You don't need a flawless lineage to lead with faith. You need the courage to stop the cycle.

You are not bound to the patterns of your past. You are not doomed to repeat what was modeled for you. You have a heavenly Father who has already defined your worth and given you everything you need to lead well.

You are not called to copy a flawed man.

You are called to follow the perfect One.

Let that become your legacy.

THREE | YOUR WIFE HAS TAKEN THE LEAD

"My wife's the spiritual one."

She prays with the kids. She reads the Bible. She's the one who gets everyone to church. So you quietly step back and think, *Why interfere with what's already working?*

But here's the truth: God didn't assign spiritual leadership based on giftedness. He assigned it based on the call.

That doesn't minimize your wife's spiritual strength. Her prayers and leadership matter deeply. But if she's carrying the full weight of leading your family toward God, it may be because you've unknowingly set your sword down.

When a man abdicates his role, someone steps in to fill the void. But that burden was never meant to rest on her shoulders alone. Even the strongest women grow weary when they carry what was meant to be shared.

Leadership at home isn't about doing everything. It's about taking ownership. It means stepping forward … not to dominate, but to serve. It's not about praying louder or teaching better. It's about being engaged. Present. Responsible.

You don't have to out-pray your wife. You don't have to become a theological expert overnight.

But you do have to show up. Because while your family doesn't need you to be flawless, they do need you to be faithful.

FOUR | NO CLEAR STARTING POINT

"I've been told to lead … just not shown how."

You've heard it before: "Be the spiritual leader of your home." But no one gave you a manual. No playbook. No real-life examples. Just a vague expectation and a lot of pressure.

So you hesitate. You freeze. You hope that one day the right moment will magically appear.

But here's the truth: Leadership doesn't start with a complete plan; it starts with a single step.

You don't need to overhaul your home in a weekend. You just need to begin.

> **Pray**—with your family, even if it's short and awkward at first.
> **Open Scripture**—reading even a single verse at breakfast makes a difference.
> **Lead in worship**—get your family to church consistently and joyfully.
> **Ask questions**—about faith, about life, about where they've seen God.
> **Let them see your love for Jesus**—not just in big moments, but also in your daily tone and choices.

Spiritual leadership isn't about knowing everything. It's about being present, humble, and willing to grow.

Your family doesn't need a theologian in the pulpit.

They need a man of God in the living room.

A man who's learning, trying, failing, and getting back up again.

The first step is often the hardest. But it's also the most important.

REFLECTION AND DISCUSSION QUESTIONS

1. Which of the four reasons has held you back the most? What would it look like to start confronting it today?

2. What small step could you take this week to begin leading your family spiritually, without waiting for permission or perfection?

FOUR SCRIPTURES EVERY FATHER AND HUSBAND NEEDS TO KNOW

You don't have to guess how to lead your family. God hasn't left you in the dark. He has spoken with clarity, and his Word provides the blueprint.

In Scripture, we're not just commanded to lead—we're shown how. With love, with strength, with humility, and with purpose.

The four passages that follow are foundational. Think of them as weapons in your leadership armory. They are truths forged by the Spirit to shape how you love, serve, and protect your family. These aren't suggestions or optional extras. They are essential.

Whether you're newly married, raising kids, or preparing for that future, these words will anchor your leadership. Read them slowly. Reflect deeply. Let them sharpen the man God is forming you to be.

ONE | EPHESIANS 5:25–33, LOVING YOUR WIFE

> Husbands, love your wives, as Christ loved the church and gave himself up for her, that he might sanctify her, having cleansed her by the washing of water with the word, so that he might present the church to himself in splendor, without spot or wrinkle or any such thing, that she might be holy and without blemish. In the same way husbands should love their wives as their own bodies. He who loves his wife loves himself. For no one ever hated his own flesh, but nourishes and cherishes it, just as Christ does the church, because we are members of his body. "Therefore a man shall leave his father and mother and hold fast to his wife, and the two shall become one flesh." This mystery is profound, and I am saying that it refers to Christ and the church. However, let each one of you

> love his wife as himself, and let the wife see that she respects her husband.

Why It Matters

This is your starting point. Not strategy. Not authority. Love.

But not just any kind of love—sacrificial love.

Sanctifying love.

The kind of love that gives, serves, and dies to self.

Paul didn't say to love your wife if she respects you, supports you, or responds the way you want. He said to love her like Christ loved the church. Christ didn't wait for the church to deserve his love. He gave himself up for her to make her holy. He led with grace. He bled with purpose.

This is the blueprint for spiritual leadership in marriage:

> *Love that initiates.*
> *Love that purifies.*
> *Love that puts her needs above your own.*

Too often, men reduce leadership to making decisions or setting rules. But biblical leadership begins with loving sacrifice. You don't lead your wife by demanding more from her. You lead by laying yourself down for her.

The call to love your wife as your own body isn't just poetic, it's practical. You instinctively care for your own needs. Scripture calls you to bring that same level of attentiveness, protection, and nourishment to your wife.

You don't lead your wife by demanding more from her. You lead by laying yourself down for her.

When you love her with Christlike love, you don't just build a healthy marriage, you display the gospel in your home.

This kind of love is your first and greatest act of leadership.

TWO | 1 CORINTHIANS 7:1–7, INTIMACY WITH YOUR WIFE

> Now concerning the matters about which you wrote: "It is good for a man not to have sexual relations with a woman." But because of the temptation to sexual immorality, each man should have his own wife and each woman her own husband. The husband should give to his wife her conjugal rights, and likewise the wife to her husband. For the wife does not have authority over her own body, but the husband does. Likewise the husband does not have authority over his own body, but the wife does. Do not deprive one another, except perhaps by agreement for a limited time, that you may devote yourselves to prayer; but then come together again, so that Satan may not tempt you because of your lack of self-control.
>
> Now as a concession, not a command, I say this. I wish that all were as I myself am. But each has his own gift from God, one of one kind and one of another.

Why It Matters

Sexual intimacy in marriage is not selfish. It's sacred.

Paul didn't present intimacy as optional or awkward. He treated it as a vital part of the marital covenant, a place of mutual giving, trust, and protection.

This passage calls men to reject both extremes: selfishness and silence. You're not called to dominate; you're called to give. You're not called to ignore; you're called to pursue with humility and honor.

Spiritual leadership includes how you approach your wife in the most vulnerable areas of your marriage. You are not entitled to her body, but you are entrusted with her heart. That means you lead by creating safety, not pressure. Pursuing closeness, not just contact. Stewarding intimacy, not just seeking it.

Paul reminds us that when intimacy is neglected, temptation grows. The enemy doesn't need a wide door, just a small crack. Leading your wife spiritually means guarding the physical, emotional, and spiritual bond that intimacy strengthens.

You are not called to just avoid sin. You are also called to pursue oneness. This is spiritual leadership where it matters most, in the hidden places. In the private spaces. In how you serve, not just how you speak.

Intimacy is more than a physical act. It is a spiritual practice of mutual sacrifice, trust, and love.

THREE | 1 PETER 3:7, HONORING YOUR WIFE

Likewise, husbands, live with your wives in an understanding way, showing honor to the woman as the weaker vessel, since they are heirs with you of the grace of life, so that your prayers may not be hindered.

Why It Matters

Peter didn't just tell husbands to live with their wives. He told them how. With understanding. With honor. With intentional care.

This verse draws a direct line between how you treat your wife and how God hears your prayers. Let that sink in.

Your spiritual leadership is not measured by your knowledge of Scripture or the boldness of your voice in public. It is measured, in part, by how gently you handle your wife in private.

Peter used the phrase "weaker vessel" not as an insult but as a call to tenderness. Like a fragile, valuable heirloom, your wife is to be treated with dignity and care … not because she's lesser, but because she's treasured. She is a co-heir of the grace of life.

To dishonor her is to dishonor the God who made her.

God does not separate your private conduct from your spiritual authority. If you dishonor your wife, your prayers are hindered. That's not a metaphor—it's a warning.

Spiritual leadership in the home begins with spiritual integrity in your marriage. And that integrity starts with how you speak to her, how you listen to her, how you protect her, and how you value her presence.

If you want to lead her well, start by honoring her deeply.

FOUR | 1 TIMOTHY 5:8, PROVIDING FOR YOUR FAMILY

> If anyone does not provide for his relatives, and especially for members of his household, he has denied the faith and is worse than an unbeliever.

Why It Matters

This is one of the strongest rebukes in the New Testament, and it's aimed directly at men who neglect their families!

Provision is more than a paycheck. It's about presence, protection, and spiritual covering. It means being there physically and emotionally. It means carrying the weight of responsibility, not just because culture expects it, but because God commands it.

Paul's words are sharp for a reason: Neglect isn't just a failure of effort; it's a denial of the faith. In other words, if you claim to follow Christ but ignore the needs of your household, your faith is exposed as hollow.

Provision means showing up. Leading when it's inconvenient. Staying steady when life feels unstable. It means sacrificing comfort to create safety and direction for those under your care.

A man forged for leadership brings stability, not chaos. Vision, not confusion. Courage, not silence. He carries the weight so others can stand taller under his leadership.

These four passages aren't inspirational ideas. They are God's design for headship in the home.

Study them.

Pray them.

Apply them.

Your family doesn't need perfection. They need a man rooted in Scripture, formed by grace, and willing to lead from his knees.

REFLECTION AND DISCUSSION QUESTIONS

1. Which of the four scriptures speaks loudest to you as a husband or father? How can you apply its principles to improve your leadership at home?

2. How do these passages change your view of being a spiritual leader in your family? How can you incorporate these teachings into your daily life to strengthen your relationships with your wife and children?

TWO PERSPECTIVES THAT REFRAME SPIRITUAL LEADERSHIP

Spiritual leadership at home doesn't start with a game plan. It starts with perspective.

Before you can lead your family with clarity and conviction, you must see two things clearly: who God is and who you are in light of him.

Most men try to lead with pressure, striving to perform, provide, and protect under the crushing weight of expectation. But when you see these two things clearly, everything shifts. Pressure gives way to peace. Striving gives way to surrender.

These truths are the framework for faithful leadership. They clarify your role, recalibrate your identity, and reshape the way you guide those entrusted to you.

Let's look at them one at a time.

ONE | YOU ARE A SON BEFORE YOU ARE A FATHER

> There is one body and one Spirit—just as you were called to the one hope that belongs to your call—one Lord, one faith, one baptism, one God and Father of all, who is over all and through all and in all. (Eph. 4:4–6)

Here's a truth that resets everything:

God is the Father. You are not.

Yes, you carry spiritual authority in your household. But that authority is not earned, invented, or self-made. It is entrusted. It's borrowed from the One who truly leads. And it's only effective when it flows from surrender to him.

When you forget that you're a son first, leadership becomes a burden you were never meant to bear. You feel the pressure to hold everything together—to be the emotional anchor, the spiritual engine, the provider, the protector, and the final authority.

But that's not your role.

You are not the savior of your family. You are a servant of the Savior.

You are a son of the Father.

And that's not weakness. That's strength.

Before you are a husband or a dad, you are a child of God. Dependent. Guided. Loved. Corrected. Covered. That's not just a doctrinal truth; that's daily fuel. Because when you understand your identity as a son, you stop leading from insecurity and start leading from intimacy.

You are not the savior of your family. You are a servant of the Savior.

You no longer lead to prove yourself.

You lead because you trust the One who is truly in control.

When a man knows he is a son, he stops trying to be the hero—and starts pointing his family to the real One.

TWO | YOU LEAD TO POINT YOUR FAMILY TO THE FATHER

> These words that I command you today shall be on your heart. You shall teach them diligently to your children, and shall talk of them when you sit in your house, and when you walk by the way, and when you lie down, and when you rise. (Deut. 6:6–7)

You're not called to be the hero.

You're called to be a guide.

That's the difference between leadership that crushes and leadership that shapes. You are not the center of your family's spiritual life. God is. Your job is to point them to him, not become a substitute for him.

Deuteronomy 6 gives us the model. Spiritual leadership doesn't thrive in isolated events. It lives in the rhythm of your day. It happens in hallway conversations, car rides, late-night prayers, and moments around the dinner table. Leadership isn't always loud, but it is consistent.

Many men get stuck here. They think leading means having the right answers. Knowing every verse. Always saying the right thing at the right time.

But that's not what your family needs. They don't need a man who pretends to be perfect. They need a man who walks with the One who is.

You're not responsible for changing their hearts. That's God's job. But you are responsible for showing them the way. For clearing the distractions. For modeling what it looks like to walk humbly, confess honestly, and trust deeply.

That kind of leadership doesn't always feel impressive. But it is faithful.

And in God's eyes, faithful is always enough.

THE FREEDOM OF RIGHTLY ORDERED FAMILY LEADERSHIP

When these two truths settle into your soul—who you are and who God is—everything shifts.

Leadership becomes less about pressure and more about peace.

You don't have to wear a cape. You don't have to fake strength or hide your flaws. You're not leading your family because you've mastered the path. You're leading them because you're walking it, step by step, under the care of your Father.

You're no longer leading to prove something. You're leading because of Someone.

This is the freedom of rightly ordered leadership:

You don't carry the full weight.

You follow the One who already carried it.

Spiritual leadership is not about being flawless. It's about being faithful. Present. Humble. Dependent.

Redirecting your family toward the grace that keeps redirecting you.

Now that the foundation is laid, we're ready for what comes next: practical action. In the next section, you'll find seven simple, repeatable steps that bring this vision to life—not just on paper, but in your living room, your schedule, and your daily conversations.

These are tools for real life.

Let's get to work.

REFLECTION AND DISCUSSION QUESTIONS

1. How does recognizing God as Father affect your role as a husband and father? How can this understanding ease the pressure to be the "perfect husband" or "hero dad"?

2. What steps can you take to lead your family toward God and integrate faith discussions into your daily routines for a stronger spiritual environment?

SEVEN PRACTICAL ACTIONS FOR LEADING YOUR FAMILY

Spiritual leadership in the home isn't complicated, but it does require intentionality. Think of it like forging a weapon in God's armory: It's not shaped by one strike of the hammer but by consistent blows over time.

You won't become a strong spiritual leader in a single moment. You will become one through steady obedience—small, intentional steps that will shape your character and strengthen your influence over time.

Think of the actions ahead like tools in God's forge. Each one is practical. Each one is biblical. And each one forms something vital in you as a man of God.

You don't need to master them all at once. You just need to begin.

Spiritual leadership in the home isn't complicated, but it does require intentionality.

These aren't lofty ideals. They're habits any man can practice. You won't find perfection here, but you will find *progress* that is measured not by applause but by your faithfulness in the quiet places where legacy is formed.

Let's step into the forge together—one action at a time.

ONE | BE INTENTIONAL

> Train up a child in the way he should go;
> even when he is old he will not depart from it.
> (Prov. 22:6)

Spiritual leadership doesn't grow by accident. It grows by intention.

Too many men hope their families will grow in faith simply by being around it. They attend church, provide for their home, avoid major mistakes, and assume that's enough. But Scripture doesn't tell us to hope our families will grow. It tells us to train them.

Training takes effort. It requires a plan. It doesn't leave formation to chance.

No soldier should enter battle without preparation. No craftsman shapes steel without vision. And no man builds a godly legacy without intention.

You don't need a perfect schedule or flawless theology to lead your family. You just need to begin on purpose.

Pray with them, even if it's short and simple.

Read a verse before dinner.

Ask your kids where they saw God working today.

Begin with a simple rhythm that places Christ at the center. These small, deliberate actions create strong spiritual grooves in the life of your home. They sharpen you. They guide your family. And over time, they forge a path the next generation will follow.

Spiritual leadership doesn't come from living with good intentions.

It comes from intentional living.

TWO | BE INQUISITIVE

When his parents saw him, they were astonished. And his mother said to him, "Son, why have you treated us so? Behold, your father and I have been searching for you in great distress." (Luke 2:48)

Mary and Joseph didn't just instruct Jesus; they also asked him questions.

Even the Son of God was engaged with curiosity and care. That tells us something important: Leadership doesn't begin with answers. It begins with presence. With questions. With listening.

As a husband or father, your role isn't simply to speak truth; it's also to draw it out. You're not just a teacher—you're a shepherd. And shepherds must know their sheep. They take time to understand the hearts entrusted to them.

Ask your wife how she's really doing. Ask your kids what they're thinking about, what they're afraid of, or where they've seen God at work. Ask what confuses them about faith or life. Questions reveal what commands conceal.

Use the in-between moments—car rides, mealtimes, evening routines—to lean in. Ask. Listen. Follow up. Don't wait for "big moments." Most discipleship happens in the mundane.

You can't lead well if you don't know what your family is carrying. And you'll never know unless you ask. Influence grows in the soil of understanding. So be curious. Ask first. Speak second. Love through listening.

THREE | BE TENDER

Fathers, do not provoke your children to anger, but bring them up in the discipline and instruction of the Lord. (Eph. 6:4)

Spiritual leadership isn't shaped by force. It's formed in tenderness.

The strongest leaders in the home aren't the loudest—they're the most self-controlled. The ones who speak calmly when the tension rises. The ones who know how to correct without crushing, to discipline without provoking, and to lead without dominating.

Paul gives clear direction to fathers: Don't stir up anger. Don't lead through fear. Instead, lead with the kind of grace that reflects your heavenly Father.

Your children are learning about God by watching how you lead. They're learning whether he is patient or harsh. Attentive or absent. Every moment of correction is an opportunity to shape their understanding of the gospel. (This isn't to put pressure on you. Remember, start small and work to be consistent.)

That doesn't mean you avoid discipline. It means you do it with care. With patience. With purpose.

Tenderness is not weakness. It's strength under control. It's strength tempered with wisdom so that it pauses instead of exploding. It's strength that restores instead of shaming.

In the forge of fatherhood, heat is necessary—but so is precision. And in the heat of the moment, the man who controls his tongue wields the sharpest sword.

FOUR | TEACH TRUTH

> He established a testimony in Jacob
>   and appointed a law in Israel,
> which he commanded our fathers
>   to teach to their children,
> that the next generation might know them,
>   the children yet unborn,
> and arise and tell them to their children.
> (Ps. 78:5–6)

Truth doesn't automatically transfer from one generation to the next. It must be taught—and lived. And the first place your children will encounter it is in you. Not just in the formal moments, but also in the everyday ones. In how you respond to stress. In what you celebrate. In how you treat your spouse. In what you do when no one's looking.

You don't need a seminary education to lead spiritually. You need to be present, attentive, and willing to bring God's Word into the natural rhythm of your home. That could mean reading a short passage over breakfast, explaining why you chose honesty in a difficult moment, or helping your child process something they saw at school through a biblical lens.

Truth sticks when it's connected to real life. And life gives you more teaching opportunities than you think … if you're watching for them.

Your children won't remember every devotional, but they'll remember how you lived. And that memory will either guide them or confuse them.

You are the first theologian your children will ever know. Let them see the truth in action. Let them see a man who not only teaches God's Word but also trusts it.

FIVE | SHARE SCRIPTURE

> Hear, my son, your father's instruction,
> and forsake not your mother's teaching.
> (Prov. 1:8)

One of the most shaping habits you can cultivate in your home is simply opening the Bible. Not in a dramatic way, not as a formal ritual, but as a steady rhythm woven into the daily fabric of family life.

Scripture was never meant to be reserved only for Sunday mornings or emergency moments. It's meant to be near. Spoken often. Recalled freely. Lived deeply.

Your role isn't to preach; it's to plant seeds. A short verse over breakfast. A scripture texted to your wife during a busy afternoon. A quiet reading before bed. These small, steady moments create a sense of spiritual familiarity. They normalize the presence of God's voice in your home.

Over time, this kind of consistency forms a biblical reflex in your family. They begin to recognize the truth. They learn how to anchor their emotions and decisions in something more stable than their circumstances. Just as importantly, they begin to hear God's Word through your voice, which makes it personal.

You don't need to be a scholar. You need to be faithful. Let Scripture be the language your family grows up hearing, not as background noise, but as a guiding light. Homes steeped in the Word become homes that stand firm when the pressure comes.

SIX | ATTEND CHURCH

> Let us consider how to stir up one another to love and good works, not neglecting to meet together, as is the habit of some, but encouraging one another, and all the more as you see the Day drawing near. (Heb. 10:24–25)

You weren't meant to lead your family alone. And they weren't meant to walk the Christian life in isolation.

Church isn't just a weekly event—it's a vital part of a spiritually healthy home. It's where your family sees faith in motion. Where they hear truth, worship together, and grow alongside other believers. It's not just a place you go. It's a people you belong to.

Hebrews reminds us that gathering with others isn't optional. It's essential. We need the encouragement, the accountability, and the shared pursuit of godliness. That includes your wife, your children … and yes, you. Leadership here begins with one simple decision: attending church. Make it a nonnegotiable rhythm. Not out of guilt or obligation, but because you believe your family needs the presence of God and the fellowship of his people.

And don't just attend—engage. Let your kids see you worship. Let them watch you serve. Let them hear you respond to the Word with humility and conviction. You're not just leading your family into a building. You're leading them into a spiritual community that strengthens what you're building at home. But far too often, weekend tournaments, youth sports, and endless events take first place—while worship takes the back seat. We're training our kids to hustle for the world and drift from the One who made them.

Families who show up regularly grow up spiritually. And leaders who walk through those doors consistently remind everyone watching—especially their children—that Christ is not an afterthought. He's the central thought.

SEVEN | PRAY FOR THEM

> Praying at all times in the Spirit, with all prayer and supplication. To that end, keep alert with all perseverance, making supplication for all the saints. (Eph. 6:18)

If leadership is a battle, then prayer is how you fight.

As a husband or father, one of the most powerful things you can do is pray for your family, not just privately, but also intentionally and consistently. Prayer is not the last resort; it's the front line.

When you pray, you're doing more than offering comfort. You're interceding. You're stepping into the gap on behalf of the people God has placed under your care. You're inviting divine strength, wisdom, and protection into their lives.

Pray for your wife's joy, her burdens, and her spiritual walk.

Pray over your children—their decisions, their friendships, their struggles, their future.

Pray for your home to be filled with peace and purpose.

And let them hear you do it. Let your children grow up knowing their father talks to God about them. Let your wife know she's covered. Your words don't have to be perfect. They just need to be seasoned with prayer.

Prayer will not always change your circumstances right away. But it will change you—and the atmosphere of your home. Over time, it will become a shield. A covering. A daily declaration that your house belongs to God.

This is what spiritual leadership sounds like in its purest form: a man on his knees asking heaven to shape what his hands cannot.

BE THE MAN WHO LEADS

Your home is more than a place to live—it's the first battlefield of your leadership and the forge of your legacy.

In this chapter, we've named the reasons men hesitate. We've uncovered the patterns—sin, shame, confusion, passivity—that hold too many back. But we've also seen something greater: a path forward.

God's Word gives us the framework. His design for the home is clear. He doesn't call perfect men. He calls faithful ones.

You've been given a charge:

> *To lead with humility.*
> *To love with sacrifice.*
> *To guide with truth.*
> *To serve with courage.*

We've walked through scriptures that shape your calling. We've explored the perspectives that reframe your identity. And we've named seven clear actions—daily, steady, simple things—that, over time, build a spiritual legacy no title or career can ever match.

So now it's your turn.

What you build in the quiet places today becomes the foundation your children will stand on tomorrow.

Take one step. Then another. Not to impress, but to be present. Not because you have every answer, but because you trust the One who does. As Charles Spurgeon once said, "Train up a child in the way he should go—but be sure you go that way yourself."

Lead by example. Walk first. Pray first. Repent first. And if you fall short tomorrow, lead again the next day. Your family doesn't need you to lead with perfection. They need you to lead with faith. Because what you build in the quiet places today becomes the foundation your children will stand on tomorrow.

REFLECTION AND DISCUSSION QUESTIONS

1. Which truth or practice from this chapter struck you hardest? Why do you think God highlighted that for you right now?

2. What step will you take this week to live out your spiritual leadership in your home, and who will you invite to hold you accountable?

HAMMER YOUR HEART: PRAYER OF HUMILITY AND SURRENDER

Exercise: Spend five to ten minutes in the evening praying a prayer of humility. Ask God to reveal areas in your life where you need to surrender and lead with more of his character. Write down any specific areas where you've felt resistance to God's leading, and commit to surrendering them.

> **Humble yourselves before the Lord, and he will exalt you. (James 4:10)**

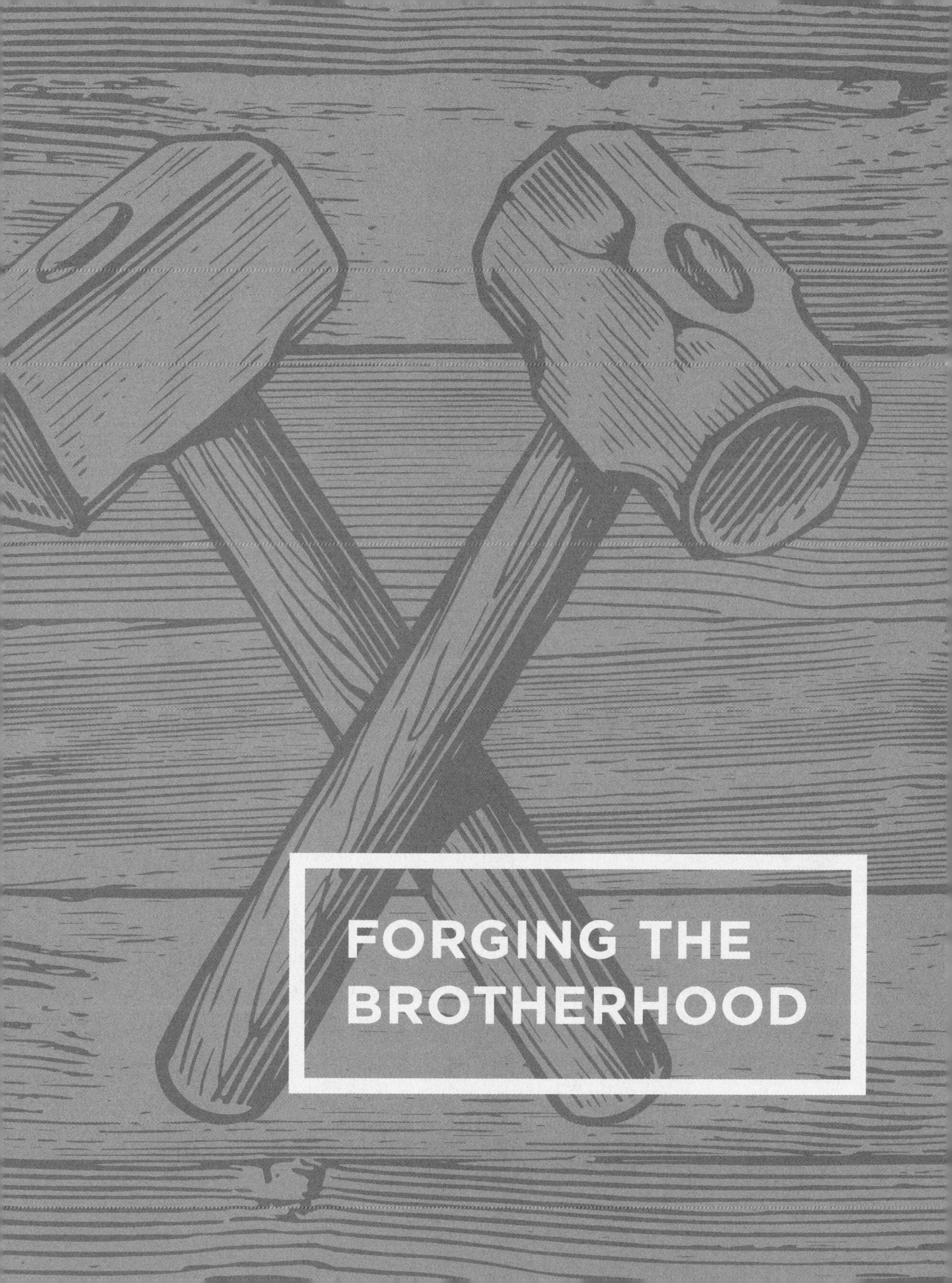

FORGING THE BROTHERHOOD

Leading at Church

For many men, the idea of leading in the church feels overwhelming.

Maybe you've felt it—that quiet tension between knowing you should step in and uncertainty about where to begin. You want to contribute, but you question your qualifications. You're not a pastor. You're not on staff. You've never been trained at a seminary. So you sit in the back row, quietly wondering, *Is there a place for me here?*

You're not alone. And you're not disqualified.

Part of the problem is that many men have inherited a narrow, distorted view of what the church is—and what leadership in the church looks like. Some view the church primarily as a building, a place where one goes on Sundays. Others view it as a spiritual service center, a space to receive teaching, encouragement, or support when life is hard. And while there's some truth in both, neither reflects the full biblical picture.

The church is not a location; it's a people. A redeemed, Spirit-filled collection of believers called the body of Christ, and you are part of it. That means church isn't just something you attend; it's also something you belong to. It's not a product you consume but people you serve alongside.

The New Testament never envisioned a church where a small handful of professionals do all the ministry while everyone else sits by and watches. Quite the opposite. Paul wrote that every believer is gifted and equipped by the Spirit for a purpose within the body (1 Cor. 12:4–7). That includes you.

And here's the hard truth: When men disengage from leadership in the church, the body suffers. When you withhold your presence, gifts, prayers, and wisdom, someone else misses out. You are not a spectator. You are part of the mission.

THE CHURCH ISN'T HERE TO SERVE YOU

Another misconception runs deep: the idea that the church exists to meet your needs.

Now, it's true that the church does bring comfort, care, and community. It should. That's part of its purpose. But if your view of the church stops at "what I get from it," you're missing the point. The church doesn't exist primarily to serve you. It exists to equip you to serve others. That's the biblical model of leadership: not consumerism, but commission.

Not "feed me," but "send me."

This was what Paul pointed to in Ephesians 4 when he said God gave leaders to the church "to equip the saints for the work of ministry, for building up the body of Christ" (v. 12). Leadership isn't about a platform; it's about preparation. And every follower of Jesus is called to the work of ministry.

Yes, that includes you—even if you've never led before. Even if you feel unsure of where you fit. Even if you've made mistakes in your past, the call remains the same: Step forward. Serve. Build. Lead. While the church may strengthen you, it doesn't revolve around you.

It's a place to grow … but also a place to give.

TWO TYPES OF LEADERSHIP IN THE CHURCH

Church leadership isn't reserved for the few—it's designed for the whole body. But not all leadership looks the same. In Scripture, we see two distinct expressions of leadership in the life of the church: *formal* and *informal*. Both are essential. Both are biblical. And both carry weight in the life of the community.

FORMAL LEADERSHIP

Formal leadership refers to the recognized, biblically qualified offices within the church, such as elders, pastors, deacons, and overseers.

These leaders are called to teach, guide, protect, and care for the flock. Their qualifications are laid out plainly in passages like 1 Timothy 3 and Titus 1. These are not casual positions. They require spiritual maturity, tested character, and a clear sense of calling.

Formal leaders bear a unique responsibility before God. They are entrusted with the spiritual care of the church and will give account for how they shepherd those under their care (Heb. 13:17). This is not a title to take lightly—but neither should it be reserved in your mind for some untouchable spiritual elite. Some men will be called to these roles. Others won't. But every man is called to lead in some way.

INFORMAL LEADERSHIP

This is where most men are called to lead and where the most impact happens.

Informal leadership doesn't come with a title. It comes with spiritual initiative. It's the man who opens his Bible in a small group and helps others understand it. It's the guy who shows up early to unstack chairs and stays late to pray with someone who's hurting. It's the quiet mentor, the faithful servant, the guy who doesn't need recognition to show up and serve.

Don't underestimate this kind of leadership. It may not attract attention, but it attracts people to Christ. You don't need to preach from a pulpit to lead in the church. You lead when you model faith. You lead when you build others up. You lead when you sacrifice your preferences for the sake of others' growth.

> **You don't need to preach from a pulpit to lead in the church.**

This is the kind of leadership Jesus modeled. He didn't climb ladders—he knelt to serve. And the church needs more men like that.

YOUR ROLE MATTERS

Whether or not you ever serve as an elder, your leadership matters. Whether or not your name appears in a bulletin or announcement, your presence matters. The men who lead well in informal ways are often the ones God uses most to shape a church's culture—because they embody quiet faithfulness.

And let's be clear: Informal doesn't mean optional.

Every man in Christ has been gifted for ministry. And the local church is the first and most important place to use those gifts. Not the last.

So ask yourself: What role am I playing in the body of Christ? Am I using my gifts for the good of the church? Or am I holding back, waiting for someone else to lead?

Because here's the truth: The church doesn't need more spectators. It needs engaged sons of God. Men who see leadership not as a title to pursue but as a towel to carry.

RECLAIMING LEADERSHIP FOR THE CHURCH

Somewhere along the way, many men stopped viewing the church as the primary place for their leadership. They show up, participate, maybe even volunteer—but the deeper calling to spiritual leadership often gets ignored or redirected elsewhere.

Instead of stepping up in the church, many redirect their gifts to their workplace, a nonprofit, or a coaching position. And while it's good (and even biblical) to bring your faith into every area of life, something is lost when your deepest leadership convictions are never applied to the body of Christ.

You weren't given spiritual gifts just to build your brand, run a business, or coach a team. You were given spiritual gifts to build the church.

It's excellent to apply biblical leadership principles in boardrooms or strategy meetings. Many men thrive in those environments—casting vision, motivating teams, solving problems. But leadership in the church is different. It's less visible. Less linear. It requires humility over hype, service over spotlight. And yet this is where your leadership matters most.

The church is not a side project. It's God's primary vehicle for advancing the gospel in the world. It's not just another place to lead. It's the place where your leadership takes on eternal weight.

LEADERSHIP PRINCIPLES WERE FORGED FOR MINISTRY

Too often, Christian men borrow biblical principles—servant leadership, integrity, sacrifice, vision—and use them to get ahead professionally, while the church gets what's left over. We apply kingdom tools to climb ladders and win influence, forgetting that those tools were never meant to elevate us … they were meant to elevate Christ.

Scripture doesn't exist to pad your résumé. It was written to shape your soul and mobilize your life for kingdom impact. Leadership in the church isn't about achievement. It's about alignment—bringing your gifts under the authority of Christ and using them to serve his body.

What if we stopped treating the church like a warehouse for spiritual content and started treating it like a training ground for spiritual leadership? What if we showed up expecting to be equipped and sent, not just fed and entertained? What if we took all our natural drive to succeed and redirected it toward serving?

Because the truth is, your leadership in the office may change a company, but your leadership in the church can change a soul, for eternity.

DON'T OUTSOURCE WHAT YOU'VE BEEN CALLED TO CARRY

It's tempting to let others lead while you hang back. Maybe you think someone else is better suited. More gifted. More seasoned. Maybe you've been burned by leadership before and prefer the safety of the sidelines. But if you're in Christ, you don't get to outsource this job.

Jesus doesn't invite just a select few into leadership. He calls every believer to participate in the life of the church. Some will lead through teaching. Some through serving. Some through mentoring or shepherding. All are needed. All are called.

And when men step up and lead spiritually in the church, everything changes.

The Word goes deeper.

Discipleship grows stronger.

The church becomes healthier.

The gospel moves faster.

You may not feel ready. Most leaders don't. But readiness isn't the point. Faithfulness is.

THE CALL TO LEAD

If you've ever felt the pull to lead in your church but hesitated because you lacked a title, felt unqualified, or thought others would do a better job, you're not alone. And you're exactly the kind of man God often calls.

Leadership in the kingdom of God has never been about titles. It's always been about calling. Jesus didn't build his church on the backs of religious professionals. He called fishermen, tax collectors, and zealots—ordinary men who learned to follow him closely, love others deeply, and lead with faithfulness.

That call hasn't changed. If you belong to Christ, you've been called into his mission. That means you're not just a participant in the church—you're a steward of its health. A contributor to its strength. A shepherd, a builder, a voice of truth, a presence of encouragement. Spiritual leadership is not reserved for the few. It is a shared responsibility for every man who confesses Christ as Lord.

Some are called to lead formally as pastors, elders, or overseers. Others lead informally as mentors, volunteers, disciplers, and encouragers. Both types are essential. Both carry spiritual weight. Both begin with the same posture: availability.

If you belong to Christ, you've been called into his mission.

And here's the key: This is not a call to platform; it's a call to obedience.

God doesn't need more ambitious men chasing influence. He desires surrendered men willing to serve. When you step into the spiritual spaces God has opened before you, something shifts. The church becomes stronger. The gospel moves with greater power. People grow. Souls are encouraged. Lives are changed.

That's what spiritual leadership does: It multiplies the life of Christ through ordinary men who are willing to lead with humility and conviction. You don't need a microphone to be a leader in the church. You need a heart that beats in rhythm with the mission of God. You don't have to be the best speaker, the most knowledgeable theologian, or the most seasoned believer. You just have to show up with a willingness to serve, speak truth, carry burdens, and grow.

Let's be clear: This will not always be comfortable. But it will always be worth it.

Leadership in the church often involves showing up early, staying late, listening closely, praying quietly, and carrying weight that no one else sees. It's rarely glamorous, but it is always sacred.

And the truth is, your church doesn't need you to be perfect.

It needs you to be present. To be engaged. To be willing. That's it. The question isn't whether you're called. (Spoiler: If you are in Christ, you are called.) The question is whether you'll respond.

This is your moment. Step into it. Not because you feel worthy, but because he is.

REFLECTION AND DISCUSSION QUESTIONS

1. How does viewing the church as a community change your involvement? How can you engage more actively in church life?

2. What informal leadership opportunities do you see? How can you serve and lead in one of these roles, even without a title?

SIX SCRIPTURES EVERY MAN SHOULD KNOW ABOUT CHURCH LEADERSHIP

Church leadership is not a title to hold—it's a trust to steward. And that stewardship begins with Scripture. The Bible doesn't leave leadership in the church up to personal preference or cultural trends. It gives us a clear, compelling framework. Whether you're called to formal leadership or faithfully serving in informal ways, these six passages offer the foundation every man needs to understand what Christlike leadership looks like in the church.

Some of these texts speak directly to elders. Others to the body more broadly. But all of them offer instruction for how men can lead well in the context of the local church—with integrity, clarity, and conviction.

These are not just qualifications to memorize. They're characteristics to cultivate.

ONE | 1 TIMOTHY 3:1–7, CHARACTER FIRST

The saying is trustworthy: If anyone aspires to the office of overseer, he desires a noble task. Therefore an overseer must be above reproach, the husband of one wife, sober-minded, self-controlled, respectable, hospitable, able to teach, not a drunkard, not violent but gentle, not quarrelsome, not a lover of money. He must manage his own household well, with all dignity keeping his children submissive, for if someone does not know how to manage his own household, how will he care for God's church? He must not be a recent convert, or he may become puffed up with conceit and fall into the condemnation of the devil. Moreover, he must be well thought of by outsiders, so that he may not fall into disgrace, into a snare of the devil.

Why It Matters

Paul began with *aspiration*—an important word. He didn't say leadership is reserved for the naturally gifted. He said it's a noble desire. But then he shifted immediately to character. Above reproach. Faithful in marriage. Self-controlled. Gentle. Not quarrelsome. Hospitable. Able to teach. A man who leads his own household well. These aren't personality traits; they're the fruit of spiritual maturity.

Church leadership must never be charisma without character. The integrity of your life is the foundation of your leadership. And before God entrusts you to lead his people, he looks at how you lead your home.

TWO | TITUS 1:5–9, HOLDING TO THE WORD

This is why I left you in Crete, so that you might put what remained into order, and appoint elders in every town as I directed you—if anyone is above reproach, the husband of one wife, and his children are believers and not open to the charge of debauchery or insubordination. For an overseer, as God's steward, must be above reproach. He must not be arrogant or quick-tempered or a drunkard or violent or greedy for gain, but hospitable, a lover of good, self-controlled, upright, holy, and disciplined. He must hold firm to the trustworthy word as taught, so that he may be able to give instruction in sound doctrine and also to rebuke those who contradict it.

Why It Matters

Paul echoed the list from 1 Timothy here, but he added a crucial element: doctrine. A godly leader must know the Word, stand on the Word, and be able to teach and defend the Word. In a culture full of spiritual confusion, men who lead in the church must be anchored in truth, not tossed by trends or preferences.

If you don't know the truth, you can't teach it. If you can't teach it, you can't protect others from error. Sound doctrine isn't a bonus for church leaders—it's a baseline. (This doesn't mean you have to be a Bible scholar or hold a seminary degree. You just have to be a student of the Word.) You may not preach from a pulpit, but every time you disciple a younger man, lead a small group, or counsel a friend, you're teaching. So know the Word, love the Word, and hold fast to it.

THREE | 1 PETER 5:1–3, SHEPHERD, DON'T DOMINATE

> I exhort the elders among you, as a fellow elder and a witness of the sufferings of Christ, as well as a partaker in the glory that is going to be revealed: shepherd the flock of God that is among you, exercising oversight, not under compulsion, but willingly, as God would have you; not for shameful gain, but eagerly; not domineering over those in your charge, but being examples to the flock.

Why It Matters

Peter painted leadership in relational, pastoral brushstrokes—not positional ones. Church leaders aren't CEOs. They're shepherds. Their authority is real, but it's exercised through service, not force.

A leader's power is not in how loud he speaks but in how well he listens, how gently he guides, and how clearly he models the heart of Christ. In God's design, influence comes through example. The strongest leaders in the church are not those who control others but those who lay down their lives for others. That's shepherding. And that's the kind of leadership our churches desperately need.

FOUR | HEBREWS 13:17, A CALL TO ACCOUNTABILITY

> Obey your leaders and submit to them, for they are keeping watch over your souls, as those who will have to give an account. Let them do this with joy and not with groaning, for that would be of no advantage to you.

Why It Matters

Leadership in the church carries a sobering weight. Pastors and elders are not just managing programs or overseeing budgets—they're watching over souls. And they will give an account before God for how they've done it.

Whether you lead formally or informally, you must remember the weight of the work. People aren't projects; they're image-bearers. And God will evaluate how faithfully you've stewarded their care. This isn't meant to scare you. It's meant to humble you ... and call you to depend entirely on the Spirit for strength.

FIVE | ACTS 20:28, WATCH YOURSELF FIRST

> Pay careful attention to yourselves and to all the flock, in which the Holy Spirit has made you overseers, to care for the church of God, which he obtained with his own blood.

Why It Matters

Paul told the elders of Ephesus to begin their leadership not with others but with themselves. Before you care for others, you must first care for your own soul. Leadership flows from your own walk with Christ. If your relationship with God is dry, your leadership will be shallow. If your character is compromised, your guidance will be confused.

You cannot give what you do not have. If you want your leadership in the church to bear fruit, it must be rooted in a private life of prayer, Scripture, obedience, and confession. The man who leads others spiritually must first be led spiritually by Christ.

SIX | EPHESIANS 4:11–12, EQUIP, DON'T ENTERTAIN

He gave the apostles, the prophets, the evangelists, the shepherds and teachers, to equip the saints for the work of ministry, for building up the body of Christ.

Why It Matters

The goal of leadership is not to impress the church but to equip it. Your job is not to do all the ministry. It's to raise up others to do it too. That's how churches grow strong. That's how disciples multiply. That's how leaders reproduce.

Every man in the church has a role to play. And leadership is about drawing that out, helping others discover their calling, sharpen their gifts, and take responsibility for their own spiritual growth. When leaders equip their team, the whole body matures.

These six scriptures provide a high view of spiritual leadership. It is rooted in character. Anchored in truth. Driven by humility. Multiplied through service. And here's the good news: You don't have to lead from a stage to live these out. You just need to lead where you are … with conviction, consistency, and Christ at the center.

REFLECTION AND DISCUSSION QUESTIONS

1. Which of these six scriptures challenges you most in your current approach to leadership in the church? Why?

2. How can you begin to intentionally model Christlike leadership among those you serve or influence?

FROM SELF-DISQUALIFICATION TO ASPIRING TO LEAD

For many men, reading the qualifications for church leadership doesn't inspire them—it intimidates them. They see phrases like "above reproach," "self-controlled," "able to teach," and they immediately disqualify themselves. Maybe that's been your reaction too.

You start thinking about the sins in your past. The seasons of struggle. The moments you lost control. The areas where you still don't feel "there yet." And just like that, you quietly excuse yourself from the calling. You believe leadership is for someone else, someone with a cleaner record, stronger theology, or better self-discipline.

But that's not how God works. Leadership in God's kingdom never begins with perfection; it begins with a willing heart. The qualifications in 1 Timothy 3 and Titus 1 aren't a report card for the spiritually elite. They're a vision for godliness. A blueprint for becoming the kind of man the church can trust. Not perfect men—but faithful ones. These qualifications aren't given to disqualify you. They're given to develop you.

GOD STARTS WITH THE HUMBLE, NOT THE POLISHED

Throughout Scripture, God consistently chooses men who feel unqualified; for example, Moses stuttered, David failed, Peter denied, Paul persecuted. Yet these were the men God used to lead his people, write his Word, and change the world.

Why? Because God doesn't start with your résumé; he starts with your readiness to surrender. He's not looking for men who have arrived. He's looking for men who are available.

Men who are teachable. Repentant. Devoted. Obedient. That's the kind of man God uses. And that's the kind of man you can become.

THE LIE OF SELF-DISQUALIFICATION

Many men carry invisible disqualifiers:

> *I've failed too much.*
>
> *I'm not smart enough.*
>
> *I don't know the Bible well enough.*
>
> *I've made too many mistakes.*
>
> *I've got nothing to offer.*

Those inner narratives are powerful, but they're also unbiblical. God never said you need a flawless past to lead. He says you need a faithful present. He never said your story disqualifies you. In fact, your scars may be the very thing that helps someone else heal. Remember, the gospel doesn't erase your past; it redeems it. And redemption is the best foundation for leadership.

PAUL'S WORDS TO TIMOTHY: LEAD ANYWAY

Timothy didn't have all the credentials either. He was young. It's likely that he was timid. Probably underestimated. But Paul still called him into leadership. Why? Because Timothy was faithful, and Paul saw what he was becoming.

> This charge I entrust to you, Timothy, my child ... [that] you may wage the good warfare, holding faith and a good conscience. (1 Tim. 1:18–19)

Timothy wasn't chosen because he had it all figured out. He was chosen because he was willing to hold on to the truth and walk in obedience. That's all God asks of you too. You may feel unqualified, but if you're in Christ, you're already called.

CHRIST QUALIFIES AND CHARACTER QUANTIFIES

Your starting point is never your track record—it's Christ's finished work. He is the one who justifies. Who cleanses. Who restores. You are not qualified by your performance but by his perfection.

But while Christ qualifies you, your character is what shapes your influence. It's how God matures you into a man others can follow. The qualities in 1 Timothy 3 and Titus 1 (faithfulness, gentleness, self-control, humility) aren't instant achievements. They're slow growth, cultivated over time through daily repentance, ordinary obedience, and God's refining grace.

So don't read those lists as a wall. See them as a path you take one step at a time, one area at a time, one conversation, one confession, one courageous act at a time.

REFLECTION AND DISCUSSION QUESTIONS

1. Have you ever felt unqualified to lead in the church? How could realizing leadership is about character and growth, not past perfection, shift your perspective and motivate you to lead?

2. Reflecting on Paul's emphasis on character, which traits do you aim to cultivate? How will you intentionally develop these traits for leadership in the church or beyond?

ASPIRE TO LEAD

The point is not to read the qualifications in 1 Timothy and Titus as a disqualification. Read them as a direction, a spiritual compass for any man who wants to live a life worthy of the gospel.

These passages aren't only for pastors or elders. They're a call to every man in the church. They give shape to godly manhood. They describe what faithful leadership looks like in everyday life—in our homes, our friendships, our churches, and our personal walk with God. You don't need a formal position to pursue these qualities. You just need a heart that's willing to grow.

So here's the challenge: Stop waiting to be perfect. Start aspiring to live the kind of life the church needs. A life formed by grace and forged by the Spirit of God.

FIVE ASPIRATIONS FOR MEN WHO WANT TO LEAD AT CHURCH

Let's walk through five key aspirations drawn from 1 Timothy, Titus, and 1 Peter. Each one is an invitation to become the kind of man who strengthens the body, leads with humility, and models the gospel.

ONE | MORAL CHARACTER AND INTEGRITY

> Therefore an overseer must be above reproach. (1 Tim. 3:2)
>
> An overseer, as God's steward, must be above reproach. (Titus 1:7)

This is where Paul started—and for good reason. Character is the foundation of trust. Without it, leadership collapses.

"Above reproach" doesn't mean you're sinless. It means you live in such a way that your life can withstand scrutiny. Your public life matches your private one. Your actions align with your confession. In short, you're not playing a role; you're living the reality.

This kind of integrity doesn't demand perfection, but it does require consistency. It shows up in the way you speak, how you treat others, how you respond under pressure, and how you carry yourself when no one is watching.

Why This Aspiration Matters

If your foundation is cracked, everything you build on it will be unstable. God entrusts leadership to men who are trustworthy. And trust is built through repentance, humility, and spiritual maturity over time.

A man of integrity doesn't hide his flaws—he owns them. He doesn't pretend to be something he's not—he invites others into his process. He leads not with pride but with a clear conscience and a soft heart.

How to Grow in This Aspiration

Start with honest reflection. Ask someone close to you (like your wife, a close friend, or a mentor) where they see inconsistency in your character. Listen carefully. Take notes. And then bring those things to the Lord.

Create regular rhythms of confession. Be quicker to apologize. Don't excuse sin—bring it into the light. Character is refined not by image management but by surrender. And remember, you don't build integrity through big moments. You build it by making the right small decisions over and over again.

TWO | FAITHFULNESS IN RELATIONSHIPS

He must manage his own household well. (1 Tim. 3:4)

[He must be] the husband of one wife, and his children are believers. (Titus 1:6)

Before a man leads in the church, he must first lead at home. Paul was clear: Your family is your first ministry. How you love your wife, raise your children, and cultivate peace in your household speaks volumes about your readiness to shepherd others.

Why? Because the home exposes who you really are.

There's no platform to hide behind. No performance to maintain. Just real life, day after day. And in that space, leadership isn't proven by power or position but by patience, presence, and consistency. You can impress people from a distance … but you shape legacy up close.

Why This Aspiration Matters

If a man cannot lead with love under his own roof, how can he lead with wisdom in the household of God? God's vision of leadership always moves outward from the inner circle: first your soul, then your family, then the church. This is not hierarchy—it's harmony. What happens in your home is not separate from your calling. It is preparation for it. Spiritual authority in the church must be anchored in relational faithfulness in the home.

How to Grow in This Aspiration

Start small. You don't need to overhaul everything at once. Schedule regular time with your wife to connect emotionally and spiritually. Create space to pray, or read a short scripture with your kids. Take the initiative in your home: Do chores and logistics with a spiritual tone.

Ask your wife and children, "How can I serve you better?" Then act on what they say.

Don't overcomplicate leadership. Sometimes the most powerful thing you can do is sit down at the table, look your family in the eye, and remind them, "I'm here for you, and I want to grow as a husband and father."

Faithfulness in relationships is forged in the ordinary, and those ordinary acts of care often have the most extraordinary impact.

THREE | FAITHFUL TEACHING AND SOUND DOCTRINE

> [He must be] able to teach. (1 Tim. 3:2)

> He must hold firm to the trustworthy word as taught, so that he may be able to give instruction in sound doctrine. (Titus 1:9)

Church leadership isn't just about leading people; it's also about leading them with truth. A man who leads in the church must know the Word of God, believe it deeply, and teach it faithfully. Paul said a man must be able to instruct in sound doctrine and refute false teaching—not as a combative know-it-all, but as a steady, trusted guide.

You don't need a pulpit to fulfill this calling. You just need conviction, clarity, and a commitment to Scripture. As I've said, if you're discipling someone, mentoring younger believers, leading a group, or even raising children, you're a teacher. The only questions that matter are these: What are you teaching, and what's shaping the message you're passing on?

Why This Aspiration Matters

We live in a time of confusion. Cultural narratives constantly reshape truth, blur morality, and undermine biblical authority. The church doesn't need more opinions. It needs men grounded in the unchanging Word of God.

If men in the church neglect sound doctrine, we don't just lose theological clarity—we lose the next generation. We drift into shallow discipleship and moral compromise. But when men know the Word and share it faithfully, the church becomes strong, stable, and spiritually secure. Teaching isn't about impressing others; it's about forming them. And that happens one conversation, one scripture, one truth at a time.

How to Grow in This Aspiration

Read your Bible every day, not out of obligation, but out of devotion. Join or start a small group where you study Scripture in community. Practice teaching the truth to others. Start with your family, friends, and coworkers. When questions arise, dig into them. Don't settle for surface-level understanding.

And don't grow in just what you know; also grow in how you share it. Learn to teach with gentleness, not arrogance. Learn to correct with patience, not pride. Learn to pass on the truth with both confidence and compassion. Because biblical leadership isn't about showing off what you've learned—it's about shepherding others with what's true.

FOUR | HUMBLE SHEPHERDING AND SERVANT LEADERSHIP

> Shepherd the flock of God that is among you. (1 Pet. 5:2)
>
> Pay careful attention to yourselves and to all the flock. (Acts 20:28)

Leadership in the church is not about being in charge—it's about being close. Biblical leadership looks a lot more like a shepherd with his flock than a general with his army. The image is personal, not positional. The shepherd doesn't lead from a distance; he walks with the sheep. He knows their names. He binds up wounds. He guides gently. He stays up when they're lost. He lays down his life when danger comes.

That's the model.

It's not a matter of leadership by domination or delegation. It's a leadership of care. And that kind of care can't be faked.

Biblical leadership looks a lot more like a shepherd with his flock than a general with his army.

Why This Aspiration Matters

We live in a world that prizes strong personalities, big platforms, and fast results. But the church isn't a company; it's a family. It doesn't need heroes—it needs shepherds. And if your leadership doesn't start with love, it won't last.

Peter warned against leading for selfish gain or out of ego. Paul echoed that the first priority is to "pay careful attention to yourself." Because a man who is disconnected from his own soul will eventually wound the souls of others. Leadership isn't about making people follow. It's about helping people flourish.

How to Grow in This Aspiration

Start where you are. Try slowing down and showing up for others. Call someone who's hurting. Pray with a brother who's struggling. Ask a young man how his walk with Christ is going, and listen without rushing to fix it. Lead a group, not as a lecturer, but as a guide. Don't aim to be impressive; aim to be present.

The most effective leaders in the church aren't the loudest in the room. They're the ones quietly carrying burdens, listening well, giving thoughtful counsel, and faithfully loving people over time. Leadership without love is just noise. But when you shepherd with humility, you don't just lead people—you walk with them toward Christ.

FIVE | SPIRITUAL MATURITY AND WILLING ACCOUNTABILITY

> He must not be a recent convert, or he may become puffed up with conceit. (1 Tim. 3:6)

> Obey your leaders and submit to them, for they are keeping watch over your souls. (Heb. 13:17)

Leadership without maturity is a spiritual hazard. That was why Paul warned Timothy not to rush men into leadership. Don't elevate them just because they're eager, articulate, or talented. A man might look ready on the outside, but if he's still spiritually unstable, leadership will inflate his pride and propel him to ruin.

The call to lead in the church isn't a reward for spiritual excitement. It's a stewardship for men who've been tested, shaped, and humbled. Spiritual maturity isn't about age or education—it's about depth, obedience, and proven character. And one of the clearest signs of that maturity is a man's willingness to be corrected.

Why This Aspiration Matters

We live in a culture that resists correction and shies away from accountability. But the church must be different. A spiritually mature man doesn't just tolerate accountability—he invites it. He doesn't hide when challenged. He grows when challenged.

If you're going to lead others well, you need people who will speak into your blind spots. You need voices that call you back when you drift. Because no one leads well in isolation. And no one drifts toward holiness by accident. Leadership rooted in pride will eventually harm others. Leadership rooted in humility will help others flourish.

How to Grow in This Aspiration

Start by identifying two or three men whom you can trust to speak truth into your life. Ask them to hold you accountable in specific areas: your marriage, your thought life, and your consistency in the Word. Don't just listen to feedback—act on it. Let conviction lead to change. Be honest about your struggles. You don't need to be perfect, but you do need to be open.

The church doesn't need more men who manage their image. It needs men who walk in the light. The man who is willing to be led is the man God can use to lead others.

IT'S TIME TO STEP INTO CHURCH LEADERSHIP

The church doesn't need more spectators. It needs men who are willing to rise—not because they have it all together, but because they're committed to growing in Christ and leading with humility.

Maybe leadership has felt intimidating to you. Maybe you've read the qualifications in Scripture and disqualified yourself before ever getting started. Perhaps you've been quietly waiting ... unsure, hesitant, or simply convinced that someone else would do it better.

But leadership in the church has never been about status or spiritual perfection. It's not reserved for the most polished, most visible, or most experienced. It's about availability. It's about obedience. It's about men who are willing to say, "Lord, I may not be much, but you can have all of me."

Paul didn't encourage Timothy to wait until he felt ready. He charged him to step up, lead faithfully, and grow into the role as he walked with God. And that same charge echoes across the generations. The invitation is not to wait until you're perfect—it's to be faithful with what you've been given, right where you are.

You don't need a pulpit or a platform to be a leader. You need presence. Start where God has placed you. Lead a men's group. Initiate prayer with a younger believer. Offer encouragement to someone who's struggling. Serve consistently, even when no one's watching. Leadership starts small. Often quietly. But over time, it builds something that lasts.

The truth is that the bench is no place for a man of God. You were never meant to sit on the sidelines and watch. You were meant to carry weight: to serve, to build, to shape, and to guide. Spiritual leadership begins the moment you decide to stop waiting for permission and start responding to the call.

The local church needs you. The next generation needs you. Your brothers in Christ need you.

And the good news is, you won't be stepping alone. You're following the One who went before you—Jesus, the Chief Shepherd, the Servant Leader, the One who gave his life for the church and continues to build it through men who lead like he did. Step in. Step up. Not for your own name, but for his. Not to impress, but to serve. Not to take control, but to be conformed. Because when you lead with a heart surrendered to Christ, you don't just make an impact for today, you leave a legacy that lasts into eternity.

REFLECTION AND DISCUSSION QUESTIONS

1. Which of the five aspirations above do you feel most called to grow in right now? What small action will you take this week to advance in that area?

2. Spiritual leaders are shaped more by their response to correction than by their natural gifts. Who are you inviting to speak into your life regularly, and how can you deepen that accountability moving forward?

SHARPEN YOUR SPEECH: INTENTIONAL CONVERSATION PRACTICE

Exercise: Each day, choose one conversation or interaction where you can intentionally speak with grace and truth. Practice speaking in a way that builds up others and reflects Christ, whether in person, on the phone, or through text or email. Record how this changes the dynamic of your day.

> **Let your speech always be gracious, seasoned with salt, so that you may know how you ought to answer each person. (Col. 4:6)**

FORGING FAITH AT WORK

Leading at Work

Most men will spend more hours at work than anywhere else. It's where we suit up daily, face pressure, chase results, and grind through challenges. But for too long, Christian men have lived as if their job and their faith belong in separate lockers—like they're carrying two identities. One for Sunday. One for Monday.

That's not how kingdom men operate. You cannot compartmentalize faith. You don't hang up your spiritual armor when you clock in. If Christ lives in you, he leads through you … wherever you are. The workplace isn't a faith-free zone; it's your front line. Your career isn't just a career—it's a calling, a battlefield, and one of the greatest mission fields in your life.

Jesus never called men to partial surrender. His call was total: "Come, follow me." That includes your desk, your tools, your meetings, and your nameplate. You don't have to preach sermons at the office, but you should live one. Every decision, every conversation, every deadline is an opportunity to reveal who rules your heart.

Many great God-fearing men have been pressured into silence about their faith at work. We fear backlash. We fear standing out. But the real danger isn't speaking up—it's blending in. Your coworkers aren't looking for a perfect Christian. They're watching for a consistent one. Integrity speaks. Humility leads. Excellence shines. And in a world starving for truth, men of God who walk with boldness and character light the way.

This chapter is about forging spiritual leadership in the workplace, about wielding your values with conviction and living so well that your life demands a gospel explanation. God has placed you exactly where you are. Not to blend, but to build.

So sharpen your edge. Strengthen your grip. The workplace isn't where your faith takes a back seat—the workplace is where your faith takes ground.

GROWING IN SPIRITUAL LEADERSHIP AT WORK

My first job wasn't exactly a hot spot for spiritual growth. I worked weekends at a mortuary, where I cleaned, answered phones, and just tried to make it through the shift. At the time, I never thought about leadership, let alone spiritual influence. I didn't see my job as a place where faith could thrive.

But over time, as my skills sharpened, jobs changed, and my faith deepened, I began to realize something crucial: Faith doesn't clock in and out. Every job became an opportunity not just to earn a paycheck but to influence the people and systems around me with the presence of Christ. I wasn't there just to perform. I was placed there by God to reflect him.

That shift in thinking changed everything. I stopped compartmentalizing my faith. I started integrating it. Like Peter said, we are "living stones … being built up as a spiritual house" (1 Pet. 2:5). That doesn't happen just on Sundays. It happens on jobsites, in offices, on sales calls, in team meetings. God is forging something eternal through our everyday work, and we're part of that construction crew.

Your workplace is not separate from your calling. It is part of your calling. Your influence doesn't have to look loud or dramatic. It starts with consistency, humility, excellence, and integrity. It looks like showing up with a Christlike presence in environments that are starving for it.

Here's the challenge: The workplace often works overtime (pun intended) to get you to separate who you are from what you do. And it's subtle. Let me show you six ways this happens:

- **Pressure**—The culture says, "Leave your faith at the door." The message is: Faith and professionalism don't mix.
- **Programming**—From school onward, we're trained to think that faith is personal and private, not public.

- **Protocols**—Company policies can imply that your spiritual beliefs are off-limits, even if they're never directly challenged.
- **Pushing**—There's often quiet but powerful pressure to conform, to go along with the crowd, and to keep quiet about your convictions.
- **Prohibition**—You may feel as if expressing your faith could cost you influence or even opportunity.
- **Persuasion**—Over time, the environment convinces you to water down your identity in Christ just to blend in.

All six of these forge a powerful cultural message that diminishes the follower's voice and forms him into cultural submission: "Faith is fine—just don't bring it to work." But that message is a lie.

Jesus never called for part-time or detached disciples. His command was total: "Sell all that you have and … follow me" (Luke 18:22). That surrender includes your identity at work—your badge, your goals, your leadership style. Following Jesus at work isn't about preaching to coworkers; it's about refusing to hide who you are in him. It's about bringing your whole self to the job and letting Christ lead through you.

This isn't about perfection. It's about presence. Your presence. His presence in you. Your workplace is not just a jobsite—it's spiritual ground and a mission field. Every interaction, every ethical decision, every moment of patience or kindness is an opportunity to reflect Christ. And the more you lean into that, the more your leadership begins to matter eternally.

Here's the invitation: Stop hiding your faith at work. Start living it. You've been placed where you are on purpose. For God's purpose. Don't waste or squander the opportunity. Your workbench is your witness stand. Pick up your tools and lead as if Christ is in the room … because he is.

WHEN I RETIRE, I'LL DO LOTS OF MINISTRY

Over the years, I've heard a familiar refrain from men frustrated with their jobs: "Once I retire, then I'll really get into ministry." It sounds noble, but it's deeply flawed. That mindset assumes that ministry starts after the job ends, when the most incredible opportunity may be in the present.

The role you hold today might be the most strategic and spiritually significant platform you'll ever have for the kingdom of God. You don't have to wait to get involved in ministry. You're already in it. As we've seen, every meeting, every project, every relationship at work is an opportunity to lead spiritually and influence others for Christ.

The workplace isn't where you just grind through the years until you can finally "do something meaningful." It's a mission field. And if we treat it like an obstacle instead of a calling, we'll miss the very assignment God has placed right in front of us.

The problem isn't that men don't want to lead spiritually; it's that we often fail to recognize our workplace as a battlefield where leadership is most needed. We've been told to keep faith private and let work remain professional. But Jesus never made that distinction. He didn't call you to a part-time ministry. He called you to full-time discipleship.

> **Jesus didn't call you to a part-time ministry. He called you to full-time discipleship.**

For this reason, we must stop compartmentalizing our spiritual life. Don't wait until retirement to "get into ministry." You're already in it. The question is, how are you conducting yourself in the workplace ministry you have? Bring your ministry to your meetings, your cubicle, your jobsite, your conference calls. You've been deployed. Right now. Where you are.

REFLECTION AND DISCUSSION QUESTIONS

1. How do you integrate faith into your daily work? In what practical ways can you express your spiritual identity at work?

2. Have you considered waiting until retirement for ministry? What ministry opportunities might you be missing at your current job? How can you act on these opportunities now?

EIGHT CHALLENGES TO FAITH AT WORK

We've seen that faith and work aren't meant to live in separate worlds. Spiritual leadership doesn't get checked at the office door. It carries into every hallway, every meeting, and every decision.

But the workplace isn't neutral ground; it's a contested space. And while it holds great potential for ministry, it also brings real opposition. That's why, before we talk about how to integrate faith and work with strength and purpose, we need to name the tension. Because living as a spiritual leader in your career is about vision as well as vigilance.

Every workplace carries pressure. Sometimes it's subtle. Sometimes it's loud. You'll face moments where your convictions will be tested, your character will be revealed, and your integrity will be on the line. Let's be honest about the challenges men face when trying to lead with faith at work and what it takes to overcome them with clarity, courage, and spiritual resilience.

ONE | ETHICAL DILEMMAS

When Faith and Compromise Collide

Every man in the workplace will eventually face moments when his faith and his job come into direct conflict. It might be subtle, like shading the truth in a report to protect a client relationship. Or it might be blatant, such as being asked to endorse a company policy that directly contradicts biblical convictions.

In these moments, the tension is real. There's pressure to go along, to keep the peace, to protect your reputation or income. But underneath the pressure is something deeper: a spiritual test. Will you compromise what's right, or will you stand firm in your convictions?

This is the challenge of ethical dilemmas. And no matter your industry or position, you'll face them. A boss may ask you to blur a number. A coworker may invite you into a dishonest shortcut. A client may expect a favor that crosses the line. Or you may simply be tempted to justify a small compromise "just this once." What makes these moments difficult isn't just the risk of consequence—it's the quiet inner battle that asks, *Is it really that big of a deal?*

Why This Challenge Matters

Ethical compromise erodes spiritual influence. It may buy you temporary success, but it costs you long-term integrity. And integrity, once compromised, is difficult to recover. More than that, ethical compromise blurs the line between who you are and who you're pretending to be. When your public role no longer aligns with your private convictions, the tension will eventually erode something: your credibility, your confidence, or your influence.

But it doesn't have to.

God never promises that standing for truth will be easy, but he promises to honor it.

> Better is a little with righteousness
> than great revenues with injustice. (Prov. 16:8)

> The integrity of the upright guides them,
> but the crookedness of the treacherous destroys them.
> (Prov. 11:3)

What Spiritual Leadership Looks Like

Spiritual leadership in the face of ethical compromise means you hold the line even when others don't. It means you choose honesty over advancement. Transparency over image. Obedience over opportunity.

This doesn't mean being reckless or self-righteous. It means making decisions that align with God's Word, even when the cost is high. Because leadership is built on trust. And trust is built on truth.

Practical Action

- **Pre-decide where your line is.** Don't wait until the moment of pressure to figure out your convictions. Know what you will and won't do before it's tested.

- **Slow down the situation.** Ethical pressure often comes with urgency. But you almost always have time to say, "Let me think and get back to you." Use that space to pray, seek counsel, and respond with wisdom.
- **Have a mentor or peer you can call.** When things feel unclear, a brother in Christ can bring perspective. Don't face hard decisions alone.
- **Let your "no" be firm but respectful.** You don't need to be combative. A calm, principled stand can speak louder than an emotional one.
- **Remember who you represent.** You don't just carry your company's name—you carry Christ's. You may not be thanked for it now, but your witness matters.

TWO | CHARACTER CHALLENGES

When Pressure Reveals the Real You

Work doesn't just shape your résumé; it also reveals your character. Deadlines, difficult coworkers, unreasonable bosses, public criticism, quiet gossip, corporate pressure—these things don't create character flaws; they expose them. And when the heat gets turned up at work, what's inside a man tends to come out.

The workplace can bring out the best in us. But more often, it reveals the parts of us that are still unformed. Pride. Envy. Control. Passivity. Anger. People-pleasing. Impatience. Fear of failure. All of these can quietly live below the surface until stress makes them impossible to ignore.

That's why work is not just a job; it's a sanctifying fire. Spiritual leadership in the workplace requires more than just competence. It requires character.

Why This Challenge Matters

Most men want to lead well at work. But you can't lead others rightly if you're not first being led by Christ. Your skill may get you influence, but your character determines what you do with it.

Unchecked character issues often start small: cutting a corner, snapping at an employee, or blaming others in a tough moment. But over time, they compound. And eventually, they will undercut your credibility and stall your spiritual influence. Character flaws that you ignore in private will always reveal themselves in public. And the people you work with (your team, your clients, your coworkers) will take notice. Leadership isn't just about what you say. It's about who you are when things go sideways.

> Keep your heart with all vigilance,
> for from it flow the springs of life. (Prov. 4:23)

> Out of the abundance of the heart his mouth speaks. (Luke 6:45)

Your heart will always show itself in your words, tone, and choices—especially when you're under pressure.

What Spiritual Leadership Looks Like

Spiritual leadership, in the face of character challenges, is being willing to be refined. It means letting God deal with your inner life, not just your outward behavior. It means you choose humility over image, confession over cover-up, and integrity over self-preservation. It also means being willing to admit when you're wrong. Apologize when necessary. And receive correction without defensiveness. You can't lead others with strong character if you're not being led into it yourself.

Practical Action

- **Notice your reactions under stress.** Do your words become sharp? Do you become withdrawn? Defensive? Ask God what these responses are revealing about your heart.
- **Invite honest feedback.** Ask someone who knows you well, "Where do you see inconsistencies in my character at work?" Write down what they say. Don't argue—listen.
- **Confess quickly and clearly.** When you make a mistake, own it. People trust a leader who repents more than one who performs.

- **Pray for formation, not just favor.** Don't ask God to just bless your work; also ask him to use it to form you into the kind of man who reflects Christ wherever you are.
- **Lead by example in pressure-filled moments.** That's when character shines … or cracks. If you stay calm, speak with grace, and act with integrity when it's hard, your influence will multiply.

THREE | SPIRITUAL ISOLATION

When You're the Only One Standing

One of the hardest things about living out your faith at work isn't the pressure; it's the loneliness. You might be the only believer in your department. The only one not laughing at the crude joke. The only one who doesn't cut corners. The only one who speaks up when something feels off. And over time, that sense of being "the only one" can wear a man down.

It's not always persecution. Sometimes it's just silence or the feeling that no one else sees the world like you do. That no one is asking the same questions, holding the same line, or seeking to live for something bigger than a paycheck.

This isolation can shrink your courage. It can numb your convictions. It can make you second-guess what you once believed boldly. And if left unchecked, it will slowly lead you to compromise, not because of pressure, but because of fatigue.

Why This Challenge Matters

No man grows strong in isolation. God designed us for community—for mutual encouragement, sharpening, and support. When you're spiritually alone at work, you're vulnerable to subtle drift. Even Elijah, one of God's boldest prophets, had a moment of despair when he believed he was the only one left. But God reminded him he wasn't. There were others, but Elijah just couldn't see them (1 Kings 19:10–18).

> Two are better than one … For if they fall, one will lift up his fellow. (Eccl. 4:9–10)

> Let us consider how to stir up one another to love and good works, not neglecting to meet together. (Heb. 10:24–25)

You weren't meant to stand alone forever. And you don't have to.

What Spiritual Leadership Looks Like

Spiritual leadership in seasons of isolation means you stay faithful even when it feels lonely. It means pressing into God when there's no applause. Holding the line when no one else is looking. Speaking the truth when it would be easier to stay silent.

But it also means seeking out community, even if it's outside your workplace. Because you need people who remind you that you're not alone. People who pray with you, sharpen you, and challenge you to keep going.

Isolation is a danger, but it's also a doorway. God can use it to refine your dependence on him. He can strengthen your convictions in the quiet. He can build something unshakable in you—if you let him.

Practical Action

- **Find one believer near you.** Look around your company or network. Is there one other Christian you could meet with weekly or monthly, even just to pray? Don't underestimate what two faithful men can do.
- **Stay connected outside your workplace.** Join a men's group, church team, or online Bible study. If you can't find one, start one. Leading doesn't mean having all the answers. It means taking initiative.
- **Feed your soul intentionally.** Podcasts, Scripture, prayer—bring spiritual oxygen into your workday, even in small doses.
- **Ask God to open a door.** Pray specifically for other believers to be revealed in your workplace. You may be surprised by who's been watching, quietly waiting for someone to speak up.

FOUR | PERSECUTION OR MARGINALIZATION

When You're Dismissed, Mocked, or Silenced for Your Faith

While some men experience outright hostility at work because of their beliefs, many more face a quieter opposition—eye rolls when they speak up, awkward silences when they share their values, or being left out of important conversations because they're "too religious."

Often, it's marginalization: subtle signals that your faith isn't welcome here. Maybe it's the promotion that never comes. The pressure to stay silent in meetings. The HR policy that contradicts biblical truth. Or the whispered jokes behind your back. It's easy to start wondering: Is it even worth it to speak up anymore?

This is where many Christian men pull back. They don't walk away from the faith—but they walk it back at work. They become functional atheists from nine to five, not because they've stopped believing, but because they're tired of being sidelined.

Why This Challenge Matters

Persecution, whether direct or subtle, tests your allegiance. And in a culture where tolerance is often demanded for everything except biblical conviction, it's becoming harder to stand for truth without a cost. Jesus warned this would happen:

> If the world hates you, know that it has hated me before it hated you.... If they persecuted me, they will also persecute you. (John 15:18, 20)

This challenge isn't new. It's normal for followers of Christ. But the temptation is to seek peace by staying silent. To blend in instead of standing firm. To protect influence (and income) by avoiding controversy. And while there must be wisdom in how we speak, there's danger in refusing to speak at all. You weren't saved to be silent. You were sent to shine.

What Spiritual Leadership Looks Like

Spiritual leadership in the face of marginalization means living with courage and conviction, even when it comes at a cost. It means choosing faithfulness over favor. Conviction over convenience. Obedience over outcome.

It doesn't mean being argumentative or confrontational. In fact, it may mean speaking less but living your faith more visibly. It means showing kindness when you're misunderstood, serving well when you're overlooked, and refusing to compromise truth even if it costs your reputation. Leadership in moments like these isn't loud. It's steady. It's men who won't be silenced, not because they're brash, but because they belong to Someone greater than the company they work for.

Practical Action

- **Clarify your convictions.** Know where you stand before the pressure comes. Write out the values you will not compromise.
- **Respond with grace, not outrage.** When marginalized, speak the truth in love. Don't fuel the stereotype that Christians are defensive or combative. Surprise people with kindness.
- **Find your boldness in the gospel.** Your identity is not your job title—it's your position in Christ. That frees you from needing approval to be faithful.
- **Remember the reward.** Jesus said, "Blessed are those who are persecuted for righteousness' sake" (Matt. 5:10). You may lose some earthly opportunities, but your eternal reward is secure.
- **Pray for those who oppose you.** Don't write them off. They may be closer to faith than you think … and your response might be the seed God uses.

FIVE | WORK-LIFE TENSION

When the Job Takes Over and the Home Gets the Leftovers

Most men don't need to be told to work hard. We're wired for it. We find meaning in productivity, we chase goals, we crave progress. And that's not a bad thing. God designed work, and doing it well honors him.

However, something happens when work starts taking up more time than it should. You stay late more often than you get home on time. You think about work even when you're with your family. You check emails during dinner. And slowly, without realizing it, your family gets the scraps.

This is the tension, not between good and bad, but between good and best. The demands of work can be overwhelming and unrelenting. And the modern world applauds hustle. But spiritual leadership means recognizing when ambition starts encroaching on the places you've been called to guard, especially your home.

Why This Challenge Matters

The workplace often rewards overextension. But God calls men to wholeness, not burnout.

Many men justify their overwork by saying, "I'm doing this for my family." But if the job consistently pulls you away from your wife, your kids, your church, and your walk with God, then the thing you're "doing for them" is actually doing harm to them—and to you. You can build a career and lose your calling. You can earn a title and lose your testimony. You can gain the world … and lose your soul.

Jesus asked the haunting question:

> What does it profit a man to gain the whole world and forfeit his soul? (Mark 8:36)

That includes the soul of your family. And the soul of your spiritual life.

What Spiritual Leadership Looks Like

Spiritual leadership in this tension means choosing what matters most, even when it costs you what the world values most. It means setting boundaries that protect your presence at home. It means making decisions not just for advancement but for alignment with God's call. It means remembering that your first ministry isn't your job—it's your home. That doesn't mean work is bad. It means work must be rightly ordered.

Spiritual leaders ask some hard questions. Is my schedule aligned with my values? Am I emotionally and spiritually available at home? Am I modeling a life of faith … or a life of fatigue? Leadership doesn't mean doing everything. It means doing the right things, faithfully and consistently.

Practical Action

- **Audit your time.** Look at a typical week: Where are you giving your best energy? Where is your family or faith being crowded out?
- **Schedule spiritual priorities.** Don't just "fit in" prayer, family dinners, church involvement, or rest. Block them like you would a critical meeting, and keep them sacred.
- **Establish daily rhythms of presence.** Create small nonnegotiables: phones down during meals, reading with your kids before bed, checking in with your spouse without screens.
- **Define success differently.** The world says success is *more*: more money, more power, more hours. God says success is faithfulness. Reframe your ambition through that lens.
- **Ask your family how you're doing.** Invite honest feedback. What do they see? What do they need? Their answers may surprise you—and sharpen you.

SIX | CONFLICTS OF INTEREST

When Your Values and Your Vocation Don't Align

Not every job is hostile to faith. But every job will eventually present moments where your convictions and your company's culture don't match.

It might be a marketing message that feels manipulative. A product that over-promises and under-delivers. A partner with questionable ethics. Or a mission that slowly drifts into territory that feels off.

At first, you may brush it off, saying, "That's just how this industry works." But over time, the tension builds. And you find yourself in a quiet inner conflict: *Can I keep doing this with a clear conscience?* This is the challenge of conflicting interests—when faith and ambition pull in opposite directions.

And if you're not careful, the slow drift of compromise will carry you further than you ever intended to go.

Why This Challenge Matters

Your work shapes your soul. And when your job requires you to set aside your convictions, even in small ways, it begins to form a divided life. You start to separate the "spiritual you" from the "professional you." You talk one way at church and another at work. You justify decisions you used to question. And eventually, it's not just your job that's out of alignment—it's your integrity.

> No one can serve two masters ... You cannot serve God and money. (Matt. 6:24)

This verse is not just about money. It's about what drives your decisions, who shapes your ethics, and what you're willing to trade for success. If you ignore these conflicts long enough, you'll either silence your faith … or leave it behind altogether.

What Spiritual Leadership Looks Like

Spiritual leadership means living a life that is undivided. It means being the same man on Monday morning as you are on Sunday afternoon. When a conflict of interest arises, godly leadership calls you to act, not in panic, but in prayerful obedience. It might mean asking hard questions. It might mean drawing a clear line. And in rare cases, it might even mean walking away from a job that no longer fits your calling.

That's not weakness. That's leadership.

A man of integrity doesn't wait until things fall apart. He pays attention early, asks bold questions, and aligns his choices with his convictions before compromise becomes his new normal.

Practical Action

- **Name the tension.** Write out the specific area where your work and your values are clashing. Clarity brings courage.
- **Talk to someone wise.** Invite counsel from a godly mentor or pastor. Ask them to help you discern whether the issue requires adjustment or separation.
- **Refuse to justify what you would never preach.** If you wouldn't recommend it to your kids or your church, you probably shouldn't be doing it. Ask: "What is this doing to my soul?" Pay attention to your conscience. If you feel uneasy, don't silence that voice—bring it to God.
- **Be willing to trust God with your career.** If faithfulness costs you a position, God is still your provider. He is not limited by the job you're in—he's forming you for something greater.

SEVEN | UNSUPPORTIVE ENVIRONMENTS

When the Culture Doesn't Encourage Your Calling

Not every challenge to your faith comes in the form of direct conflict. Sometimes it's the slow erosion of living in an environment that doesn't support, value, or even acknowledge your spiritual life. You're surrounded by good people—hardworking, talented, maybe even kind. But faith is never mentioned. Spiritual priorities are seen as irrelevant. And talking about Jesus? That feels like introducing a foreign language in the boardroom.

The danger of this kind of environment isn't hostility; it's apathy. And over time, apathy can be just as dangerous to your faith as persecution. When no one around you reinforces your beliefs, your convictions start to feel strange. You don't abandon your faith; you just stop feeding it. You stop bringing it up. You stop praying during lunch. You stop being the spiritual presence God called you to be. And before long, your light dims—not from pressure, but from passivity.

Why This Challenge Matters

We were never meant to follow Christ in isolation. We were built for spiritual reinforcement, for rhythms of encouragement, and for mutual sharpening. But in many modern workplaces, that reinforcement simply doesn't exist. That doesn't make you a victim, but it does mean you'll need an intentional strategy.

Jesus warned us not to hide our light:

> You are the light of the world. A city set on a hill cannot be hidden.... Let your light shine before others, so that they may see your good works and give glory to your Father who is in heaven. (Matt. 5:14, 16)

Even when no one celebrates your faith, your presence still matters. In fact, your quiet integrity, your work ethic, your patience under pressure, and your care for people might be the most powerful testimony they ever encounter.

What Spiritual Leadership Looks Like

Spiritual leadership in unsupportive environments means being anchored in private so you can stand strong in public. It means developing spiritual habits that don't depend on external encouragement. It means keeping your spiritual candle lit, even when no one's watching. It means choosing to engage rather than withdraw.

You may be the only Bible some of your coworkers will ever read. So make your life legible. Not through perfection, but through consistency, presence, and purpose. You don't have to shout. You don't have to argue. You just have to show up with the Spirit of God alive in you.

Practical Action

- **Build private habits that fuel public strength.** Start your day in the Word and in prayer. Even five minutes can re-center you for the battles ahead.
- **Let your faith show in natural, humble ways.** Pray before meals. Mention your church casually. Speak truth with kindness when someone asks for advice.
- **Don't wait to be asked: Be available.** Unsupportive doesn't mean uninterested. People will notice your life long before they inquire about your faith. Be ready when they do.
- **Look for spiritual allies.** Is there a quiet believer in the office? Someone who shares your values? A connection like that can refresh your spirit in dry environments.
- **Remember why you're there.** You weren't placed in that job just for a paycheck. You're a light, even if you feel alone. You may be the one God sent to prepare the soil.

EIGHT | PRESSURE TO CONFORM

When Culture Pushes You to Fit In Instead of Stand Out

Every workplace has a culture. And whether it's shaped by success, speed, image, or innovation, there's usually an unspoken expectation: Get on board. Fit in. Don't make waves.

And while some of that is normal and even healthy (such as alignment, collaboration, and shared goals), the danger comes when those expectations push against your convictions. You start noticing what gets rewarded: self-promotion, spin, shallow leadership. You feel the pull to match the energy of your peers, even if it's not godly. You begin adjusting your tone, hiding your values, silencing your faith—not because anyone told you to, but because it's easier that way.

That's the pressure to conform. And it rarely shows up in a dramatic moment. It's a thousand tiny choices to blend in when God's called you to stand apart.

Why This Challenge Matters

Conformity is comfortable—but it's also costly.

Paul said it plainly:

> Do not be conformed to this world, but be transformed by the renewal of your mind. (Rom. 12:2)

When you conform, you trade transformation for acceptance. You choose peace over power. And eventually, you stop looking like salt and light, and you start looking like everyone else.

Here's the danger: The more you conform outwardly, the harder it becomes to hear the Spirit inwardly. And before long, you forget what it felt like to walk with boldness and conviction.

What Spiritual Leadership Looks Like

Spiritual leadership in a culture of conformity means living with quiet courage. It means knowing what you believe, why you believe it, and to whom you ultimately answer. You don't need to be abrasive to stand out; you just need to be anchored. Anchored in Scripture. Anchored in identity. Anchored in Christ. That kind of man doesn't shift with the winds of popularity or policy. He stands with grace, speaks with clarity, and lives with conviction—regardless of the cultural cost. He may not be the loudest voice in the room. But his life will speak volumes.

Practical Action

- **Clarify your nonnegotiables.** Know the lines you won't cross and why. Write them down. Pray over them. Revisit them often.

- **Speak with wisdom and restraint.** Not every situation requires a speech, but some require a stand. Learn to discern the difference.
- **Surround yourself with voices of truth.** Podcasts, Scripture, mentors, and brothers in Christ. Keep the truth louder in your life than culture.
- **Practice spiritual resistance.** Say no when everyone else says yes. Walk away when a compromise is expected. Your quiet resistance will leave a mark.
- **Remember who you represent.** You don't carry the name of your company above all. You carry the name of Christ. Let that guide your posture and your decisions.

FORGE IN THE FIRE OF WORK

BRINGING IT ALL TOGETHER

Work is not just what you do; it's where who you are is tested, shaped, and revealed. And if you're serious about following Christ, then you can't afford to leave your faith at the door Monday through Friday. The workplace is a forge. It will test your ethics. Expose your character. Challenge your convictions. Confront your comfort. And sometimes leave you standing alone.

But it's also where God forms spiritual leaders.

The fire you face at work is not meant to destroy you—it's meant to refine you. The eight challenges we've just walked through (ethical dilemmas, character formation, isolation, marginalization, overwork, conflicts of interest, unsupportive environments, and pressure to conform) are not interruptions to your spiritual growth; they are the context in which God is growing you.

They're not distractions from ministry. They *are* ministry.

Each challenge is a chance to reflect Christ. Each moment of pressure is a moment to practice obedience. And each decision to stand firm when it would be easier to give in is a declaration that Jesus, not your job, is Lord.

You may not get applause. You may not get a raise. But you will gain something greater: godly resilience, a clear conscience, and a legacy of faithfulness that echoes far beyond your office walls. So don't shrink back: Step forward. God placed you in your workplace for more than a paycheck. He placed you there to be a light, a leader, and a man who brings his presence into the ordinary.

And now, we make a shift. As important as your spiritual leadership at your job is, God never meant for that leadership to stop at the workplace.

You've been forged in the home.

You've been equipped in the church.

You've been tested at work.

Now it's time to shape your influence in the wider world around you. There's a circle of people—friends, neighbors, teammates, golf buddies, old classmates—who are watching your life. They may never set foot in your church, but they're already in your orbit. The question is: What kind of influence are you having there?

In the next chapter, we'll turn our attention to your circle of influence, those everyday relationships where spiritual leadership often begins not with a sermon but with a conversation. Not on a platform but over a backyard fence.

Let's talk about how to lead in the spaces where your life speaks the loudest.

REFLECTION AND DISCUSSION QUESTIONS

1. Think back to a time when your integrity was tested on the job. How did you respond, and what did it reveal about your readiness to lead spiritually in difficult situations?

2. When your workplace feels spiritually dry or isolating, how do you stay grounded in your faith? What practical steps can you take to build community, encouragement, and accountability—even outside your job?

TEMPER YOUR EMOTIONS: REFLECTION AND RESPONSE

Exercise: Reflect on one situation each day this week that stirred up a strong emotional response. Take a moment to pause and assess whether your reaction was led by emotion or guided by the Spirit. Write down your thoughts and adjust how you can respond in a more godly, stable way moving forward.

> **"In your anger do not sin": Do not let the sun go down while you are still angry, and do not give the devil a foothold. (Eph. 4:26–27 NIV)**

FORGING YOUR CIRCLE

Leading in Your Relationships

Influence used to be simple.

It was earned over time—built in neighborhoods, through church gatherings, over backyard fences, and on sideline bleachers. Men led by proximity. Their presence was known, and their word carried weight because it came from a life people saw firsthand.

But in today's world, that kind of influence feels like an endangered species. Our lives have become more fragmented. We scroll more than we speak. We know someone's highlight reel but not their heart. The conversations that once took place face to face now hide behind filters, emojis, and polite digital distance. As a result, the kind of spiritual influence that grows through real, life-on-life connections is fading.

The good news is that the need hasn't changed—and neither has your calling. You're still surrounded by a circle. It may be smaller. It may look different from what it did in previous seasons. But it's just as strategic. In fact, in this cultural moment, it may be more sacred than ever.

You have influence in places a pastor may never be invited. You have access to hearts that won't respond to a sermon but will notice your life. The question isn't whether you're a leader in your circle—it's whether you're paying attention to it.

Your gym crew. Your golf foursome. Your fantasy league. The dads on your kid's team. The coworker you grab coffee with every other Friday. These aren't just acquaintances; they're opportunities. They are your front line of ministry.

> Look carefully then how you walk, not as unwise but as wise, making the best use of the time, because the days are evil. (Eph. 5:15–16)

You don't need a title or a theology degree to lead in your circle. You need better things: availability, consistency, and conviction. You need the Spirit of Christ alive in you. And you need to see your daily routines as divine assignments.

This chapter is about reclaiming the overlooked places in your life—the informal spaces where genuine trust is built, real influence occurs, and true leadership is required. It's about stepping into your circle not just as a friend, neighbor, or coworker but as a man sent by God, armed with truth, grace, and spiritual grit.

So look around. Who's within arm's reach? Who laughs at your jokes, takes your advice, and texts you when life gets sideways? Who trusts your presence, even if they've never asked about your faith? That's your mission field. That's your circle. And God placed you there on purpose.

You don't need to be loud. You don't need to be famous. But you do need to be faithful.

You don't need to be loud. You don't need to be famous. But you do need to be faithful. Spiritual leadership in your circle won't be built through grand gestures but through daily presence, intentional living, and a willingness to speak when it counts. This is where discipleship begins. In backyards, break rooms, and on barstools. In early-morning workouts and late-night texts. In your circle.

Let's look at how to lead there—with clarity, conviction, and Christ at the center.

THE MINISTRY OF THE MUNDANE

WHERE ORDINARY MOMENTS CARRY ETERNAL WEIGHT

We often assume that real ministry happens somewhere else: on stages, in pulpits, on mission trips, or behind microphones. But some of the most powerful spiritual work God does isn't in the extraordinary. It's in the everyday.

Jesus modeled this. His first miracle wasn't in the temple—it was at a wedding in Cana. He didn't call his disciples from seminaries, but from fishing boats and tax booths. He taught by asking questions around dinner tables, turning walks into lessons, and flipping interruptions into divine encounters. He noticed Zacchaeus in a tree. He talked theology with a woman drawing water. He restored Peter by a charcoal fire after breakfast. Time and again, Jesus leveraged mundane settings to achieve an eternal impact. That's not by accident. It's by design. Because that's how influence is forged.

Most of your life happens in the ordinary: commutes, meetings, grocery runs, texts, pickup games, and parking lots. That's where leadership takes root. Not because of how impressive you are, but because of how present you are.

> Whatever you do, in word or deed, do everything in the name of the Lord Jesus. (Col. 3:17)

The man who brings spiritual intentionality into everyday spaces becomes the kind of leader God can trust with greater influence. Why? Because he's not performing. He's practicing faithfulness when no one's watching, and that kind of faith makes a mark.

Your circle doesn't need to hear grand speeches; it needs a man who shows up. A man who listens more than he lectures. A man who asks questions that open hearts. A man who prays, even silently, as others speak. A man who lives consistently so that when crisis strikes, people know who to call. That's spiritual leadership in the mundane.

So the next time you're standing around the grill with your crew, or waiting for the next tee time, or sitting in the stands on a Tuesday night, don't underestimate the moment. These times may seem forgettable. But in the hands of God, they can become sacred.

THE POWER OF CONSISTENCY

If presence is the beginning of influence, consistency is what makes it stick.

Influence isn't earned in a moment; it's earned over time. It's the result of doing the right thing so many times that people can't ignore the pattern. It's the man who keeps showing up, who says what he means and means what he says. Who's dependable in the storm and anchored in his convictions.

And in a world of constant turnover, flaky commitments, and fleeting attention spans, consistency is rare—and powerful. It doesn't mean being perfect. It means being present repeatedly. It means following through when it's easier to cancel. Choosing to encourage when sarcasm is the norm. Praying for a friend without needing applause. Refusing to drift into disengagement just because life gets busy.

Consistency builds trust. Trust builds influence. And influence builds legacy. So if you want to shape your circle, don't underestimate the power of doing the same good thing over and over with joy and humility. Over time, it will speak louder than any onetime display ever could.

A BIBLICAL PATTERN FOR SMALL-CIRCLE INFLUENCE

This kind of circle-based leadership isn't a modern work-around. It's a biblical pattern.

Jesus, the greatest leader of all time, modeled it. He spent most of his ministry not in crowds but with a small circle. He had twelve disciples but invested most deeply in just three: Peter, James, and John. And of those three, John is described as the disciple "whom Jesus loved." That's a model of tiered influence: the many, the few, and the one.

The apostle Paul followed the same pattern. He preached publicly, but he discipled Timothy and Titus personally. He traveled with tight-knit ministry teams. And when he wrote his most personal letters, they were often to individuals, not churches.

In Acts 2, we are told that the early church met "day by day, attending the temple together and breaking bread in their homes" (v. 46). Ministry wasn't confined to big spaces. It happened around tables, in homes, and within relationships that carried weight.

You don't need a microphone to have a ministry. You just need a circle and a commitment to be spiritually present inside it.

You don't need a microphone to have a ministry. You just need a circle and a commitment to be spiritually present inside it. This biblical pattern leads us to one clear conclusion: Spiritual leadership doesn't begin with a platform—it begins with faithfulness in your circle.

SPIRITUAL LEADERSHIP STARTS SMALL

WHY FAITHFULNESS IN THE LITTLE THINGS MATTERS MOST

We often evaluate leadership in terms of size: how many people we reach, how visible we are, or how much impact we have. But in God's economy, influence doesn't start with scale. It starts with stewardship.

> One who is faithful in a very little is also faithful in much. (Luke 16:10)

Spiritual leadership begins with the small things, because that's where character is forged. And the truth is, most men don't stumble in the spotlight—they stumble in the shadows. It's not usually the big moments that take men out; it's the small, daily compromises that go unchecked.

But the reverse is also true: When a man shows up faithfully, even when no one notices, God sees. When he chooses prayer over pride, service over self, or truth over convenience, God sharpens him. And when he treats a casual conversation with the same intentionality as a Sunday sermon, God multiplies his impact.

Some of the most influential leaders you'll ever meet aren't the ones up front. They're the ones behind the scenes. They don't lead large crowds; they disciple one man at a time, week after week, coffee after coffee. They invest quietly, consistently, and intentionally. And they leave legacies.

So, before you aspire to reach many, ask yourself: *Am I being faithful with a few?*

Do I follow through on my words?

Do I show up when I say I will?

Do I pray for my circle by name?

Do I lead even when it's inconvenient?

It's not glamorous. But it is godly. And that's what God honors. Think about Jesus again. He spent most of his public ministry with twelve men. Sometimes with three. He healed crowds, yes, but he discipled only a few. He didn't go viral; he went deep. And so should we.

Your influence in your circle won't be measured by how many people you impress but by how many lives you've faithfully invested in. And that starts with one text. One visit. One bold but gracious conversation. One prayer no one hears ... except God. Small faithfulness builds deep trust. And deep trust opens the door to lasting spiritual influence.

WHAT LEADERSHIP LOOKS LIKE IN REAL LIFE

Let's make this tangible.

You're at the gym. A guy you see every Tuesday opens up to you while wiping sweat from his face. He mentions trouble at home—his marriage feels cold, and he's not sure it'll make it. In that moment, leadership is less about quoting Scripture and more about asking a meaningful question: "Have you talked to God about it?" Or maybe just: "Want to grab coffee later this week?"

You're at a neighborhood firepit. A few jokes get crude. One guy laughs loudest. Another glances your way. He knows you're a man of faith. Do you chuckle along to fit in? Or do you steer the conversation in another direction? Sometimes leadership means changing the subject. Sometimes it means walking away. And sometimes it means staying so that someone else can see what it looks like to stand firm.

You're on the sidelines at your kid's game. A dad next to you gets animated. The ref made a bad call. He mutters something ugly under his breath. You nod and say, "It's a tough call, but he's doing his best." You just modeled self-control. It doesn't feel like a sermon. But to the watching eyes of that dad—or maybe your own kid—it might've been one.

These events aren't theoretical. They are all real events that happened to me. It is here, in these small moments, that we realize leadership isn't standing behind a podium. It's staying with a pattern. And the more you let your faith shape your ordinary responses, the more extraordinary your influence becomes.

WHEN YOUR INFLUENCE GROWS

STAYING GROUNDED WHEN GOD EXPANDS YOUR REACH

Spiritual influence is often quiet at first, even unseen. But as you live faithfully and lead with integrity, something begins to shift. Your circle watches. People lean in. Trust grows. Questions come. And suddenly, your influence widens. This is the moment many men don't expect.

Such men weren't grasping for influence. They were simply trying to be faithful in their friendships. However, others are now asking them for advice. Others are watching how they live. Others are starting to follow their lead. It's a gift, but it's also a test. When God expands your influence, it's not for your platform. It's for his purpose.

> Let the one who boasts, boast in the Lord. (2 Cor. 10:17)

The danger in spiritual leadership is not just failure; it's also success. Influence can quietly inflate ego. Visibility can blur identity. And the admiration of others can make you forget why you started leading in the first place. But remember: You're not the hero of the story. Jesus is.

You're not building your own kingdom—you're stewarding his. That's why growth in influence must always be matched by growth in humility. As more people look to you, the more you must look to Christ. So when your voice begins to carry more weight in your circle:

> *Stay tethered to Scripture.*
> *Stay honest with your brothers.*
> *Stay prayerful in your planning.*
> *Stay low, even when others lift you up.*

The more visible your leadership becomes, the more invisible your dependence on Christ must remain. When others look to you, don't point them to yourself. Point them to the source. You are not the answer. You are the pointer arrow.

> He must increase, but I must decrease. (John 3:30)

When your influence grows, stay grounded. Let humility be your posture. Let the Word be your compass. Let Christ be your goal. Because the man who stays grounded in Christ will never be shaken by influence.

REFLECTION AND DISCUSSION QUESTIONS

1. Where has God already given you consistent influence, and how can you become more intentional about leading in that space this week through presence, words, or action?

2. Are there any subtle ways that pride or hesitation has kept you from stepping fully into spiritual leadership? What would it look like to lead with greater humility and boldness in your current circle?

THREE MATTERS THAT SHAPE YOUR CIRCLE

HOW YOUR CONDUCT, SPEECH, AND PRESENCE FORGE SPIRITUAL INFLUENCE

Spiritual leadership isn't about wearing a title. It's about how you live when no one's asking for a sermon but people are still watching your life. And your circle of influence? That's the front line. It's where leadership is either forged or forgotten.

You don't have to be a pastor, speaker, or Bible scholar to lead. You just have to be consistent, intentional, and present. Every group you're part of—your gym buddies, neighbors, coworkers, or golfing crew—is an opportunity. In every circle, you carry influence. The only question is how you're wielding it.

Influence in your circle shows up in three distinct and powerful ways: your conduct, your speech, and your presence. These are your everyday weapons. Your personal armory. And how you handle them shapes the spiritual climate around you.

ONE | YOUR CONDUCT MATTERS

People notice how you act long before they care what you believe. That's why Paul wrote:

> Let your manner of life be worthy of the gospel of Christ. (Phil. 1:27)

Your behavior is your witness—especially when no one's handing out awards for it. At the driving range, a guy in your group shanks ten balls and starts unraveling. Do you laugh? Feed the frustration? Or keep it light, calming the energy, showing there's another way to handle pressure?

Or say your rec league team just lost a close game. The ref blew a call. Emotions are high. Everyone's watching your response. Do you mutter under your breath or walk over and thank the ref anyway?

These are the micro-moments when leadership is quietly forged. Conduct isn't about having spotless behavior; it's about being steady and grounded when others are unhinged. Choosing humility when pride would be easier. Staying honest when no one's watching. That's leadership people remember.

Sometimes leadership is what you *don't* do. When the guys start trash-talking their wives, complaining about church, or mocking someone behind their back, do you go along? Stay silent? Walk away? You don't have to preach. You just have to live in a way that makes people wonder what's different about you. And when they do, you'll be ready to answer.

TWO | YOUR SPEECH MATTERS

Your words are a double-edged sword. They can build up or tear down, bless or burn. Paul exhorted:

> Let your speech always be gracious, seasoned with salt. (Col. 4:6)

Salt preserves. Salt purifies. Salt enhances. Your words should do the same. You're out to lunch with a few coworkers. The conversation turns political or religious, and the tone turns sharp. Do you throw fuel on the fire? Or do you slow things down, redirect the conversation, and let grace season your tone?

Sometimes it's what you say that changes the room. Other times it's what you don't say. Maybe you're out boating, and someone drops a crude joke. Do you laugh along to fit in? Or stay quiet, signaling by silence that you live by a different code?

Your speech, spoken or withheld, shapes the room. It reveals who's forming your identity: Christ or the crowd. So speak life. Speak the truth. And when necessary, say nothing at all. Because sometimes silence leads louder than a sermon.

THREE | YOUR PRESENCE MATTERS

Presence might be the most underrated form of leadership. You don't always need words. Just showing up speaks louder than anything you could say. In the Bible, when Job lost everything, his friends sat with him in silence for seven days (Job 2:13). No advice. No platitudes. Just presence. That still matters.

You get a text—someone just lost a loved one. Do you freeze, unsure about what to say? Or do you show up at the service, offering quiet solidarity? That act of presence will be remembered far longer than anything you could have said.

Also, sometimes leadership means not showing up. A party, a weekend trip, a happy hour—the kind that'll likely go sideways. Your gut says don't go, so you don't. That decision may say more than your presence ever could.

Then there are the smaller but sacred moments: helping someone move, showing up for the weekly group, checking in with a buddy who's gone quiet. It's not flashy, but it's faithful. And faithfulness is what influence is built on. Presence says:

> *"You matter."*
> *"I see you."*
> *"I'm here when it counts."*

That's leadership people trust.

LEAD WHERE YOU ARE. NOW.

THE CIRCLE AROUND YOU IS WAITING

You don't have to be further along. You don't need a title. You don't need to wait for a sign. You already have influence. Right now. Right where you are.

The people in your circle already trust you. They laugh with you, text you, show up in your life. They may not call it discipleship, but they're watching you, listening to you, and absorbing how you live.

> The harvest is plentiful, but the laborers are few. Therefore pray earnestly to the Lord of the harvest to send out laborers into his harvest. (Luke 10:2)

You are one of those laborers. And your circle is your field. Your gym buddies, your coworkers, your brothers-in-law, your weekend crew—they are your current assignment. Not someday. Today. Not somewhere else. Here. Not someone else. You.

And this isn't about perfection; it's about presence. It's not about having all the answers. It's about showing up, speaking life, living faithfully, and loving people well. So here's the charge: Lead where you are. Open your eyes to the people already around you. Listen more. Encourage often. Speak truth when it counts. Show them Christ … not through a sermon, but through a consistent, surrendered life.

You're not just a golf partner.

You're not just the guy in the group text.

You are a man of God.

And your influence—when wielded with humility and faith—can shape hearts, redirect stories, and ripple into eternity. That's how legacies are forged. One conversation. One prayer. One decision. One life at a time.

LEGACY IS LOCAL

When most men hear the word "legacy," they think big. They imagine stadiums, platforms, foundations, or movements. But real legacy doesn't usually begin on a stage. It begins in a circle.

It begins with a teenager who watches how you treat your wife. A neighbor who notices your joy in hardship. A coworker who sees you show up early, stay late, and never cut corners. A friend who remembers that you prayed when no one else knew what to say.

Your legacy won't be written in headlines—it'll be etched into hearts. Your influence may not trend, but it will transform. Because the most powerful legacy isn't passed down through speeches. It's passed down through faithfulness. Through presence. Through integrity when no one's clapping.

So don't underestimate what God is doing through your ordinary obedience. Don't wait for a larger stage. You already have one. It's your circle. And if you lead well there, you may shape legacies that echo far beyond your lifetime. In the end, it won't be the crowd that counts. It'll be the circle you led with faithfulness.

REFLECTION AND DISCUSSION QUESTIONS

1. Which of the three matters in this chapter—conduct, speech, or presence—do you most need to sharpen in your current circle of influence? What is one way you can lead more intentionally this week?

2. Think of one relationship or group you're in all the time. How can you reflect Christ more clearly in how you act, speak, or show up, even when no one's asking you to?

STRENGTHEN YOUR PRESENCE: BEING FULLY PRESENT

Exercise: At some point during the day, practice being fully present in a conversation or interaction with someone. Put away distractions, listen intently, and engage with that person in a way that reflects Christ's attentiveness. Afterward, reflect on how your presence impacted the interaction and how being present can help you lead in your circle.

> **Love one another with brotherly affection. Outdo one another in showing honor. (Rom. 12:10)**

FROM THE FORGE TO THE FIGHT

Your Call to Lead

IT'S YOUR TURN

Brother, we've come to the end of this journey together, and I want you to hear this clearly: Your time to lead is now. The world needs men who stand firm, men who lead in their homes, workplaces, and communities, and who aren't afraid to show up, even when it's hard. What I've shared with you in these chapters isn't just for the pages of this book—it's for the real world, where the battle is fought every single day.

Every area of life is a battleground, and every man is called to rise up. Whether it's in the quiet moments with your family, the challenging interactions at work, or the friendships that need a godly influence, you have the armor to lead. Don't wait for the "right time"—the time is always now.

I know it can be easy to get caught up in the weight of your responsibilities. It can feel like the challenges are too big, and maybe you've disqualified yourself from leading. But listen to me: God has equipped you for this. The armor of faith, integrity, and character that you've been called to wear is not heavy; it's empowering. Your faith is not just something you carry on Sundays—it's the weapon you wield every day, everywhere you go. Whether it's holding firm when the pressure is on, speaking life into others, or just being a presence that reflects Christ, you are more than capable.

I've talked about a lot of areas where you can lead, and you might be feeling overwhelmed. Maybe you're wondering, *Where do I start?* Or maybe you've already been leading in some areas but feel like you're not seeing the impact you desire. Here's the truth: Even small steps are victories. Your influence matters, even when you can't see it yet. Every choice you make to lead with integrity, every word you speak with grace, every moment you show up for someone—these are not insignificant. They ripple out, impacting lives in ways you might never fully know.

Now, as we close this book, I want to remind you that this is not the end of the journey. It's the beginning. This is where the rubber meets the road, and where your leadership will be tested in real time. There will be challenges: times when you doubt yourself, when you want to pull back, when the enemy whispers that you're not enough. But I want you to remember this: You are enough. God has called you, and he will strengthen you.

So armor up, my friend. The world is waiting for men like you. Men who lead with courage, who stand firm in faith, who speak truth, and who show up when others are sitting on the sidelines. You don't need to be perfect, you don't need to have it all figured out, and you don't need a stage. You just need to lead where you are.

PRAYER OF COMMISSIONING

Father, we stand before you as men who are ready to embrace the calling you have placed on our lives. We ask for your strength and courage to lead in the places you have assigned to us—whether in our homes, our workplaces, our churches, or our communities.

Lord, forge us into the men you have designed us to be. Refine our hearts, sharpen our character, and give us the wisdom to lead with integrity and humility. Help us to be men who live out our faith authentically, who speak truth with grace, and who are present when our influence is needed most.

We commit to leading with purpose, not for our glory, but for yours. We trust in your power to shape and equip us for every challenge that lies ahead. As we step into this battle, we pray that you would empower us with your Holy Spirit, protect us from the enemy, and help us to honor you in every action, word, and decision we make. In the name of Jesus, we commit our leadership to you. Amen.

Vince Miller

vince@beresolute.org

651-274-8796